C000063E_6

HIDDEN LIGHTS

HIDDEN LIGHTS

Ordinary Women, Extraordinary Lives

Joan Blaney

HILLCROFT COLLEGE
LI... ...E RESOURCES
... ...Y BANK
SURBITON
SURREY KT6 6DF

BlackAmber Books

Published in 2001 by
BlackAmber Books
PO Box 10812
London SW7 4ZG

1 3 5 7 9 10 8 6 4 2

Copyright © Joan Blaney

All rights reserved.

The moral right of the author has been asserted.

No part of this publication may be reproduced, stored in a retrieval system
or transmitted, in any form or by any means, electrical, mechanical,
photocopying, recording or otherwise, without prior permission
of the publishers.

A full CIP record for this book is available from the British Library.

ISBN 1–901969–05–3

Typeset in 11/13 point Horley Old Style
by RefineCatch, Bungay, Suffolk
Printed and bound in Finland by WS Bookwell

For my dearest daughter,
Siobhán Marie Blaney

'A young woman of substance'

Contents

Acknowledgements

Special thanks to my mother, Virginia Smith, Mary Blaney and Dorrie Parsons; to my father, Samson, my brother, Solomon, my sisters, Lorna, Rosalee, Pearl, Yvonne, Sharon and Diane, and my nieces and nephews.

My thanks, too, to Katrin Wolf, Eric Adams, Peter Stokes, Derek Douglas, Kim Newcombe, Joan Starbuck, Andy Goode, Andy German, Barbara Trevail, Elizabeth Etti, Joyce Sidhu, Margaret Geary, Ralph and Chris Smith, Matthew Pike and all the other people who encouraged and helped me to achieve one of my lifetime ambitions in writing this book.

Many thanks to the Barrow Cadbury Trust, the Lord Ashdown Settlement and the Mill Dam Trust for their support.

Lastly, and above all, my heartfelt thanks to the women whose stories appear in this book, for taking me into their confidence and trusting me with some of the most enthralling aspects of their lives.

Foreword

Barbara Follett

Women are better survivors than men, and certainly better at coping with adversity. I will defend this assertion to anyone, and I will use Joan Blaney's book as evidence.

While the stories of Joan of Arc and the Duchess of Devonshire grab political headlines, it is the day-to-day bravery of women like Mary Seacole, Emmeline Pankhurst and the heroines of *Hidden Lights* that really proves my point. In this small volume Joan sums up women's ability to rebuild themselves, their families and their communities, no matter what the world throws at them. From Northern Ireland to South Africa, and right around the globe, Joan shows how women make strong and determined contributions to their societies.

The historians may not have written about ordinary women much, focusing more on the glamorous and glamour-seeking, but the bravery they have ignored is woven into the fabric of history and is here shown in a sharp, bright light. The ten women whose stories are told are not film stars or pop icons; they are the real story of feminine success, and they are the women who set the example for the next generation. I hope that when others read this book, and learn of the obstacles that women all over the world have had to overcome, they will be given the confidence to achieve their personal goals.

The three stories of women from South Africa are particularly poignant for me because of the years I lived in that country, witnessing the oppression of apartheid and the vicious impact it had on individual lives. Surely, without the dogged determination of South Africa's women, from the groups of politically active women to the mothers of Soweto, apartheid would not have been overturned? And Vesta's story, and her struggle to help the victims of abuse and sexual attack today, shows how women keep moving forward, not settling back because one political or social barrier has been overcome. There is always more we can do, and it is usually the women who see what needs to be done.

Anyone who reads this book will become aware of the contribution that has been and can be made by individual women everywhere. The stories are inspiring because they show women working on their own initiative, using their own experience and getting results. They show politicians like me the way forward – that putting laws on the statute book is not enough. We need to empower people at every level to make lasting changes to the daily lives of all in our varied communities. I have met many accomplished and influential women, but few have been as inspiring as those in this book.

Of course, Joan Blaney herself should be part of this book because she is part of the female success story. As founder of Women Acting in Today's Society (WAITS) and now as development director for the Scarman Trust, she has made a terrific contribution to a worldwide network of women's groups.

Joan has been part of important international programmes to give women a sense of self-worth through community-based action. She has helped women set up businesses, gain employment, get educated and get funding. She has helped individual women understand themselves better and to take on positive identities. And she has helped gain ever more recognition for women's role in making the world a saner – and safer – place. This book is another milestone on the long road towards full recognition and appreciation of women's achievements, and Joan is one of the leaders of the trek.

London, November 2000

Introduction

'No one can make you feel inferior without your consent.'
Eleanor Roosevelt

During my working life I have been privileged to meet with some remarkable people. Now, as I look back, I recognize that, in the main, it is the women I encountered who have influenced me most.

When I was training to become a nurse at the Queen Elizabeth Medical Centre in Birmingham, I was fortunate to work alongside women such as Sister Collette Clifford and a Jamaican auxiliary nurse named Agnes Patterson. As well as helping me through my course, they provided me with examples of humility, dedication and love, even when faced with the most difficult situations. Although many other fine people worked at the Queen Elizabeth, there was an indefinable quality about these two women that I greatly admired.

Some time later, after the birth of my daughter, Siobhán, and a new career with a local authority, I became acquainted with the ideals of feminism when I found myself challenging racist attitudes in the workplace. It seems only common sense now, but back then it was something of a surprise to discover that the same people and structures that discriminated on grounds of race also did so on grounds of gender. The experience was revelatory, as well as hurtful, and I became driven to work in the voluntary sector, to try and put right some of what I felt was socially wrong.

1

Within ten years, I had established two charities, the second being a Women's Organization called Women Acting in Today's Society (WAITS). During my work with WAITS, I made contact with many women from Europe and South Africa and learnt that there is indeed a 'universal woman's experience'. So many of the issues that confront women in Britain are also faced by women in Europe and Africa. Of course there are differences in culture, outlook and ethos, but there is a richness in that diversity. In many ways the things that set us apart are outnumbered by the things we have in common.

Over the last few years, I have been moved and inspired by the women I have met during my travels. Whether it is a woman who struggles daily to bring up a child with severe learning disabilities or one who goes to prison in the cause of freedom, in both cases their strength and determination are clear for all to see. The woman who helps those who are younger and less privileged shows the same sort of compassion as the woman who helps her fellow refugees. The Jew, the Muslim, the Christian and the non-believer all strive in their own ways to achieve social justice.

Not only have I been moved and inspired, but I have been humbled that these women have entrusted me with their stories, revealing, in some cases for the first time, their most painful experiences. There were times when we cried together and times when we laughed; times when I was made to understand the power of women and the power of love.

History is often recorded by the victors, and more often than not it is men writing about men. I suppose that has been one of my main motivations to write this book and, in doing so, to challenge those representations. While it is easier to catalogue big events in the annals, and to record history as a series of events which feature a relatively small number of characters, it is my contention that history is far more complex than the actions of a few political and military leaders. It is the actions of countless millions of people that have formed the world as we know it, and for the most part their stories remain unrecognized outside their own communities. The contributions that women have made remain, with a mere handful of exceptions, hidden; the chroniclers rarely allow their talents to shine through the pages of historical texts. With this deficiency in mind, I have chosen to write about the lives of ten so-called 'ordinary women', to enable their struggles and their triumphs to light a path which others may choose to follow.

The first reaction of the women of whom I write was often: 'Why me?' or 'I have done nothing really' or 'I feel guilty, because I know of other people who have achieved much more than I have.' Most of them tended to play down their own achievements, while praising those of others.

Despite the geographical distances between them, and the differences in the societies in which they work, there are striking similarities. For example, I found that the model of feminism I had grown accustomed to in Britain is not readily accepted in Africa or Eastern Europe. Perhaps that is because the women featured in this book, when they found themselves in situations of conflict or revolution, were often already disadvantaged because of their race, religion, political persuasion, status or class. Each disadvantage they faced as women was only one more barrier they had to overcome.

None of these women is a 'superwoman'. Like the rest of us they have all felt anger, fear, vulnerability, the need to be recognized and the need to be loved. They have made mistakes and have failed in some of their endeavours. For the most part, they did not set out on a crusade but, because of a twist of fate, found themselves in circumstances in which they were confronted by injustice. Like the rest of us, they would have preferred an easier life:

there were the heavy demands of family and work; there were many excuses available to permit them to look the other way. However, they did not look away. Somehow, they found the resolve to match the compassion that enabled them to act in a way that changed their own lives and the quality of life of the people around them.

The latter part of the twentieth century saw great political upheaval, and women and children usually bore a disproportionate amount of the suffering as the dust settled in the aftermath of such events. When faced with adversity, all the women of whom I write have displayed many of the same virtues.

It is easy for me to imagine that the campaigner for freedom in South Africa would have acted in a similar fashion to the woman born in East Germany and vice versa; that the Sudanese refugee in England and the Jewish woman from the Ukraine who now lives in Germany share many attributes. That the white English Christian and the so-called coloured Muslim woman from Johannesburg, who are both involved in the care and education of small children, have almost identical values. Their achievements cannot be either classified or graded, because it was the circumstances in which they found themselves that dictated what was required of them. The important thing is that they refused to accept the status quo, refused to be victims: they saw what needed to be done and did *something*.

I am grateful that they have shared their experiences with me and have given me the hope that every woman may be able to take something positive from this book.

Elsie Saunders

1 The Hand that Rocks

Wolverhampton is an industrial city of 250,000 people a few miles north of Birmingham, in the midlands of England. It was once famous for its heavy industry and the Wolves Football team, which was one of the best in Europe in the 1950s. But, like its industry, the glory days of its soccer tradition have faded into the distant past.

In the aftermath of the local MP Enoch Powell's notorious 1968 'rivers of blood' speech against immigration, Wolverhampton, with its multi-racial population, acted as a barometer for race relations in Britain. In observing what was taking place in the town, Tony Benn, one of the most renowned left-wing politicians, was moved to comment, 'The flag of racialism has been raised over Wolverhampton.'

Like many other towns and cities, Wolverhampton did have its problems, but in no way did it descend into the bloody strife predicted by Powell and some of his colleagues.

In the latter part of the twentieth century the town centre was rejuvenated and the worst of the housing has been renovated or bulldozed; some of the more unpleasant memories were buried under the rubble. On the surface, Wolverhampton has become a place more at ease with itself. But, despite the new roads and buildings, one does not have to dig too deep to find many of the social problems common to large metropolitan areas throughout Britain.

*

Oblivious and seemingly untouched by such problems, the laughter and cries of small children reverberate round the local community centre. They clamber on the small climbing-frames or push themselves about in colourful plastic cars. Away from the hurly-burly, a few young mothers sit around on chairs in corners, some with other children on their knees, talking about their everyday experiences of motherhood. The centre is in The Scotlands, an estate which suffers from poor housing and high unemployment. Its reputation is one of deprivation, and in the past it has been one of the most crime-ridden areas of Wolverhampton. The shortage of leisure and recreational facilities leaves toddlers playing dangerously on busy streets, while their mothers, many in need of advice and support, ponder their future in isolation.

Elsie Saunders sits in one corner of the hall, her intelligent blue eyes taking in all that is happening around her. She radiates a calm which seems to slow the children who pass close by her and they lower their voices from high-pitched excitement to low reverential tones when they address the slim woman with silver-grey hair. Elsie is of mature years and she is separated from the young women by at least two generations. Although from the same area, she was born into a world far removed from what the young women have experienced. She grew up in a community where running water, an inside toilet and electricity were the stuff of fabulous luxury, not the rudimentary necessities for a decent life that are the rightful expectation of people living in Britain at the dawn of the twenty-first century.

Throughout her life, Elsie has sought to change not only her own circumstances but also those of people around her. In many instances the changes she has striven for and achieved seem unremarkable to those who take their rights and roles in British society for granted. But what has been achieved by women campaigning for equality has been built on the lives and work of many women like Elsie Saunders, mainly on their refusal to accept the status quo and their determination to achieve their goals. Their lives could be described as a string of relentless and mundane struggles which have resulted in countless small triumphs that have collectively and steadily changed society's priorities. By their example, they have not only altered how women see the world around them but also transformed how women see themselves.

Elsie checks her watch. She is only visiting the centre, because she runs a similar Carers and Toddlers group and a playgroup a few miles away. It is time for her to leave for the playgroup, and she stands and waves her goodbyes to the young women. They respond with good-natured enthusiasm and call out that they will see her again soon. There is much Elsie can teach the young women, who have come together out of their loneliness, but she waits to be asked. They have a respect that is mutual.

Elsie was born in Tipton, part of England's industrial heartland known as the Black Country, so called because its heavy industrial base emitted an all-pervasive acrid smog which coated buildings with a layer of soot. The area was sometimes called the engine-room of the British empire, as almost everything imaginable made from metal, whether steel, copper or brass, had its origins within the blackened walls of the factories of Tipton and surrounding areas such as Bilston, Dudley, Walsall and Wolverhampton.

Elsie's family background like that of the majority of people in the area was industrial. Her father had worked in a foundry and her mother in a munitions factory.

'I was the second of three children,' she says. 'I had an older sister named Joan and my parents later adopted my younger sister, Brenda.'

Elsie grew up in a country that experienced great social changes in the aftermath of the Second World War. The

Labour Party came to power in 1945 and for the first time in its history it had a big enough parliamentary majority to introduce measures which were to lift millions of British people from abject poverty. While the creation of the welfare state and the provision of a free and comprehensive national health service were welcomed, opinion polls showed that the issue that most concerned people was housing. Under Clement Attlee's government, Labour's greatest – and probably least recognized – achievement was the construction or renovation of one million houses and flats.

'We lived in a council house, and in those days council houses were seen as a step up the social ladder when compared to the old houses that were available from private landlords.

'We weren't very well off, but it didn't really matter if you were poor because you always knew someone who was poorer. We would often share what we had and everybody looked after one another.'

Although roles were subtly changing in postwar Britain, there were some that remained well defined in the community in which Elsie lived: fathers were the breadwinners and mothers stayed at home to look after the children. Children under ten years of age also had their allotted tasks.

'When I was nine, every Sunday morning I had to take a trolley to the gasworks to collect coke – which was left after the gas had been taken out of the coal – to burn on our own fires. The trolley was a box with two handles and two wheels. I had to go a mile and a half with this trolley, and had to push it over the railway crossing, down the other side and round a corner.

'I would start out at six a.m., and would sometimes have to stand in the queue for about an hour before collecting around a hundredweight of coke which was extra to our rations of coal.

'Most of the time it was freezing, and we didn't have warm clothes. But worse than that was when the trolley wheels fell off as they very often did, especially when I was pushing it back up the hill.

'Children worked very hard in those days fetching the shopping and doing the housework, which included scrubbing the floors and putting red polish on the doorsteps. We did a lot of this, sometimes before we went to school and even during our lunchtimes.

'We were brought up in a culture of hard work, but we didn't mind too much because we were a happy family. There was no television and so we listened to the radio and played cards and dominoes. Both my parents played the piano and the accordion. My sister Joan played the piano. I loved music and always enjoyed the evenings when we would gather around the piano and have a good old singsong.

'We didn't worry too much about anything because we knew that whatever our parents did they were doing for the best.'

Elsie's family was one of the first to benefit from the programmes that aimed to provide every house in Britain with proper water and sanitation services, but having a bath still required much preparation and co-ordination.

'Boiling water would be poured into a bathtub that was on the hearth and families would go from the cleanest first to the dirtiest, who would be the last in the bath. I used to love going in after my big sister, because she was working and would buy luxuries like scented bath cubes. I would spend as long as I could in the bath after she got out, just so that I could soak up the perfume.'

Elsie considers herself lucky that she did not come from one of the large families that were common in the area. The scarcity of resources not only led to a restriction in the frequency of bathing but also meant it was usual for the washing of clothes, a burdensome task for women in those days, to be limited to once a week.

'Saturday or Sunday nights were bath nights and then we would have a clean vest and a pair of blue panties that would have to last for the week. It was only if we were going on a school trip or visiting the doctor that we changed. We didn't have wardrobes because we didn't have the clothes to put in them. A chest of drawers was enough.'

Leisure pursuits for young women of Elsie's social standing were limited to trips to the cinema, dancing once a week, or a visit to the youth club. It was unacceptable for a woman to go into a pub, even with her boyfriend, and smoking in public was frowned upon. But despite the restrictions, when she was fifteen Elsie did manage to meet the young man who was to become her husband.

'A friend and I had been sitting on a park bench when we saw these two lads cycling around the bandstand. It took them a while before they came up and asked us for a date. I liked Reg straight away. He was tall, with dark hair, and had a very nice smile. Even so, they had to ask a few times before we eventually agreed to go out with them. If someone asked you out you weren't expected to say yes straight away; if you did, you were considered "forward".'

Courting couples like Elsie Longford and Reg Saunders had to go to many lengths to be alone. 'Transport wasn't easily available and you would often have to walk miles to see your chap. But you didn't do it for the exercise!

'When Reg and I were courting I had to be in by nine o'clock and if I was late my dad would be standing on the doorstep waiting for me. Reg had to be off the premises by 9.30 p.m. and if he didn't go sharply my mother would shout to me, "It's time you came in or he'll miss the bus." It might seem intrusive to young people today, but that is how it was for us and we accepted it. Our parents made the rules and we stuck by them.

'I was married at eighteen and had my first child at twenty. This was a respectful period between the time of my marriage and the birth of my child, so that no one would think that I got married because I was pregnant. Such a thing would have brought shame on my family.'

Marriage did not make life much more comfortable for Elsie and Reg, as they were married at a time when there was still rationing of basic foodstuffs like eggs, butter and sugar, a situation that continued until 1952.

Their first marital home was a one-bedroom bungalow which they rented from a private landlord.

'It was a small place. We had no electricity and had to rely on the noxious and sometimes dangerous town gas, as opposed to the cleaner, safer and natural gas that is piped into houses today. Gas provided heating and lighting and we were only able to cook on one single ring. Washing in those days was a chore. I would first have to put heavily soiled clothes into the coal-fired boiler, then wash them in a tin tub before putting them through a mangle to get rid of most of the water. Washing would take many hours, and sometimes a full day for women who had a family of small children.

'We used flat-irons, and I had two that I took from my mother's house because she was only using them for door-stoppers. I would put one on the hearth and the other on the gas ring to heat it up. To test whether the irons were hot enough to use, we would spit on them. If the spit bubbled and rolled off, they were ready. If you were more cultured, you would probably sprinkle water onto the iron from a bowl.'

Young newly married couples were expected to be frugal and to purchase only the bare necessities. Elsie and Reg's main wedding gifts were tablecloths, pillowcases and towels. Most of them came from coupons which families and friends had saved up. Money remained scarce in the early years of their marriage. Although there were opportunities to add to the goods they had received, this could not be done without the prying eyes of neighbours.

'When we got married, catalogues, from which you could buy things by weekly payments, was what a lot of people used. But you couldn't tell anyone that you had bought something from a catalogue because there was a stigma attached to buying things you couldn't pay for. It was the same with hire purchase. Some people bought things from the tallyman, who used to go from door to door selling household goods on credit, which they paid off at a few shillings a week, but you wouldn't talk about this, either, because you felt embarrassed.

'Mind you, people only commented if they saw you with things they knew you couldn't afford, and so I would only buy bed linen from the catalogue. I'm sure that we had the best-made beds in our street.'

It was expected that married women would bear children and there was often subtle pressure from family and peers for the marriage to prove 'fruitful'. Bringing a child into the world was not just a matter for the two parents, because a member of the extended family frequently carried out postnatal care.

'After giving birth, especially to your first child, you would have to stay in hospital for up to eight days and then at home for up to two weeks. Your mother's friend would come around to look after you, mainly because your mother was busy looking after your younger brothers or sisters. You did as you were told and there was no taking the baby up the street in a couple of days like you see young mothers doing today.'

In the late 1950s there was something of an economic boom in Britain and Reg, Elsie's husband, moved from his job in the warehouse of a rolling-mill to a better-paid post as a maintenance worker. This improvement in their finances enabled them to move to a two-up, two-down house, with electricity, in 1958. By this time Elsie was working at home, tracing industrial drawings of pumps from paper to linen. It was a wise move by her employers to provide the implements and the means by which she could continue to work from home, because Elsie was a skilful and committed worker and they did not want to lose her. It was also a way of working which fitted well with Elsie's other responsibilities and provided her with an opportunity to realize one of her many dreams.

'I used to work late into the evenings and, with the money I earned, after five years we were able to put a deposit on a house being built on a site in Coseley, a small village between Bilston and Tipton. Reg and I used to visit the site as the foundations were being laid. Sometimes the whole area was under a blanket of smog from the nearby metalworks. But this didn't worry us too much, because we wanted the house. The smog and the factories, unfortunately for many people who lost their jobs at the time, have all disappeared but we are still living in our little house.'

It was Elsie's idea to buy a house, which was a rarity for people of her upbringing, and Reg took some persuading. Eventually they became the first property-owning members of either family. In a modern context this move may seem nothing extraordinary but at a time when the class structure remained rigid and all-pervasive, Elsie's attitude and actions were a radical break from a mindset that restricted both ambition and opportunities for people from humble social and economic backgrounds. In her own small way, Elsie was playing a part in the social revolution that had begun in postwar Britain.

Not long after they moved into their new house, Elsie had a second son and, taking advantage of a life made much easier with the advent of washing-machines and other modern appliances, she decided on a more challenging career.

'For as long as I can remember I always wanted to be a

teacher. I was recommended for grammar school, but my parents couldn't afford to send me, and so I went to Park Lane Secondary Modern for Girls and started in the second year. I had no problems keeping up with the work but missed out on music lessons, which I would love to have done, because they were only taught in the first year.'

Only two jobs were available for girls leaving a secondary school at that time: work in the local factory or in the fish shop. Elsie's teacher, recognizing her talents, which would have been wasted in either job, found her a post as an office junior in the drawing-office of a local company called Lea Howl Pumps. The manager, Mr Snowdon, quickly spotted Elsie's abilities and she was moved to work on the drawing-boards.

As a young mother, Elsie joined her local Young Wives group and, inspired by the weekly meetings and discussions, she decided that, with both her sons at school, she would set out to look for a new career. She went to her local college to ask about a teacher-training course and felt dejected when told that she required five O levels to enter the course. It was with some sadness that Elsie reflected on having left school with no qualifications, a matter made worse when she considered that she could have got the required qualifications if only she had been able to take her place at the grammar school.

After sharing her disappointment with a friend, Elsie took her advice and went to another college where a nursery-nurse course was being run.

'My friend was already a qualified nursery nurse and made the job sound interesting. When I inquired about the training I was told that I needed two O levels, and I said I would like to do three.

'I was taken aback when I heard that each O level would take up to two years and that I would be expected to do a total of six years at night school. I simply said that as a mature student I didn't have six years to spend gaining three qualifications. The course tutor said I could do them in three years if I was to put my mind to it and so I decided that I would go ahead.

'I took English language and literature. It was in the seventies and sociology was the subject everyone was taking at that time, and so I did that as well.'

Not every member of the family was enthusiastic about Elsie's new venture. In many ways, it appeared that men tended to be more accepting of their positions while women strove to improve their lot. This invariably created some tension between Elsie and Reg, but she had her own way of dealing with it.

'My husband is very good and always helps with the housework. But on the evenings when I had to go to night school, he wouldn't do anything. That was his way of expressing his disapproval. I was a little upset at first because I really would have liked to know that I had his support, but in the end I just left him to get over it and he did.'

Elsie passed her three O levels in half the allotted time and subsequently got a place on the two-year nursery-nurse course at Dudley College of Further Education. Her tutor had warned her that the course would be as arduous as training to be a teacher but she was not going to be discouraged.

'Having done my O levels I had the taste I needed to study and I was very excited at the thought of doing more. Many of my friends and relatives thought I was mad and that I wouldn't do it, but I was determined.

'Being a mature student I didn't want to look out of place when I started college and so asked a friend if she knew what the kids were wearing. She told me that I needed to buy an expensive pair of jeans and then rip them below the knees and that I was to wear an old sweater with holes in it. This seemed a strange idea to me, especially when I had spent time darning my sons' jeans.

'In the end I wore what I wanted to. I was a student and had no worries about going along with my group to the refectory during the break times.'

As Elsie settled into her course the workload increased and so did the pressures at home.

'My son Jonathan was studying for his O levels at the time that I was on my course, and books and files were piling up all over the house. I know that Reg wasn't happy, and when they started to stack up in the lounge it simply got too much for him.

'He decided to put a floor in the attic and all my books and folders were banished up there. When I needed my books, I had to take the ladder to get them, but I didn't mind this because it was a good compromise. I was so wrapped up in my studies that I didn't see how much that was impinging on our lives. In his own way Reg was trying to help, and I was grateful to him for that.'

Elsie's mother, Sarah Longford, was concerned that her daughter was taking on too much. Furthermore, nobody known to the family had ever studied at night school before or had shown the level of ambition Elsie had. It was hard for her to accept that Elsie was to become a pioneer in a community where aspirations were best described as fairly modest. Sarah also felt that she might be an extra burden on her daughter.

'My mother was a forthright and independent woman who taught us all to read and I remember when we used to read together as a family. In some way I guess that I got much of my determination from her. After she had been diagnosed with cancer of the colon, she had a colostomy and was given only eighteen months to live. She lived for eighteen years.

'Even though my mum had a home help, she didn't want them to do her washing and so I did it. This wasn't a problem for me, because our parents had looked after us and it was our turn to look after them.

'Halfway through my studying, my mum's condition worsened and she died. She had wanted to see her grand-children grow up and get married. She didn't quite manage that, but it had been enough to keep her going for so long.'

Following the death of her mother, it was left to Elsie to look after her father, David Longford. She was in the final year of her course, the amount of course work had greatly increased and she began to feel the strain. Her elder sister then suggested that their father should move in with her.

'My father living with my sister would not have worked, because my dad was the kind of person who liked to have his own way and needed his independence. I felt that he would be able to look after himself as long as he had help and decided to give up my course. When I told him what I was going to do, he was very upset with me and said, "My wench, you've got to carry on".'

It was hard for David Longford to cope without the woman he had been married to for fifty years, but he persevered. Wanting not to be a burden and to take some of the strain from his daughters, he not only did what he could for himself, but also found that a new world opened up for him when he began to venture out to places of interest, using his bus pass. Elsie was pleased that her father had been able to preserve his dignity and independence by becoming self-reliant.

The days of studying, some of which started at five in the morning and went through to midnight, ended in September 1977 when Elsie passed her final examinations and became a qualified nursery nurse.

'I owe a lot to my tutors, who gave me excellent support and encouragement, and to my husband and children. Reg was quietly pleased and came with me to collect my certi-ficate. My children were also pleased that their mum had done something with her life. It was not as much as I could have done if I'd had the chance, but I had achieved my goal. I believe that if you have to stop and think about opportunities you have lost, you will never get anywhere.'

After two years of studying, Elsie decided to take a few months' break to catch up with the housework and other things that she had neglected, before embarking on her new career.

Jobs in her new field were hard to come by and after months of disappointments, sometimes without a response to job applications, she decided to do some voluntary work.

'My training had involved spending time in college with the course work and some time at a local nursery. I felt it was important to keep my hand in, and so decided to go back to the nursery where I trained, to work as a volunteer. It was there that I saw an opportunity for paid work.'

The Education Department in Dudley had a list of supply teachers and Elsie approached the chief officer to find out if there was a similar list of nursery nurses. There wasn't and he was not receptive to her suggestion that they start one.

'I explained that if a nursery nurse was away a teacher was expected to stand in, and would not be able to give the kind of attention little ones would need and deserved, as well as do their own work.

'He was adamant that such a list of supply nursery nurses wasn't required, but I was persistent and suggested that he should think about it and that I was prepared to go to any nursery in Dudley, as long as I knew the day before. I gave him my contact details and then left.

'Nothing came of it for a few months but when a member of staff at the nursery where I was volunteering was away, he phoned and said, "Here's your chance." I took that chance, and stayed on supply for eighteen months.'

The supply idea worked and a list was established, providing newly qualified nursery nurses throughout the borough with opportunities where none had previously existed.

But this was not the first change that Elsie had engineered.

'One of the jobs I had applied for was working with children at a special-needs school. They had a swimming-pool and I was asked what I would do if a child were in danger in the pool. I said that I couldn't swim but would do everything to grab the child and shout for help.

'I didn't get the job because I couldn't swim. I went back to my tutor and suggested that they made sure that people attending the course could swim or that they introduced swimming as part of the course. They did both.'

Although Elsie enjoyed supply work, she continued to apply for a permanent position: with the experience her supply teaching had provided, she felt that she should have been able to secure one. Furthermore, she could not accept that her application was not even good enough to warrant an interview. Frustrated but not discouraged, she tried a new tactic.

'When I was training, a lot of people thought, first of all, that I was too old to be starting a new career, and secondly that I was entering a field which was considered to be more appropriate for younger people. Because of this, I decided that I would not include my age on the application form but simply write, "Over twenty-one".

'Shortly after this, and by some weird coincidence, I received a telephone call which invited me for an interview and I got the job.

'When I started, the woman in the personnel department said I had not completed the form because I had failed to include my age. I told her that it was deliberate and not an oversight.'

Even now, Elsie refuses to state her age, feeling that in British society people are judged by their age and not by their experience, interest or ability to do a job. Once again, and in her own inimitable way, Elsie Saunders has made a stand against the prejudices of society.

Settled in a more permanent position, Elsie felt better able to plan her work, attend to her family's needs and care for her elder sister, Joan, who had had a series of strokes.

'This was quite a difficult time for me, because heart problems are hereditary in my family. My father, mother and sister all had the same problems of diseased valves and I myself am considered to be at risk. It was a lot for me to take on at the time, and I know that Reg was a little worried.

'After her operation, my sister had two strokes. Each time she recovered she needed a little more care, because she had lost her speech and then the full use of her right arm and her right leg.

'But like my mum Joan was a fighter, and at one time, when she was in a wheelchair, she learnt to knit using only her left hand. I admired her courage and it was a very sad day for me when she never fully recovered from the third stroke that finally killed her.'

Elsie's father, too, had a series of strokes and had to be moved to an old people's home. She visited every day and brought in extra food, having watched him go from eleven stone (154 pounds) to nine stone (126 pounds). Just as he was beginning to gain weight, he had another stroke and died.

After twenty or so years of a career in nursery care, Elsie decided to take early retirement. But, as so often in her life, she viewed the closing of one door behind her as an opportunity to open another one in front. The next was to lead to another phase of voluntary work with children and their mothers on the Old Fallings estate in Wolverhampton.

Elsie was brought up in the Church of England, and although Reg was a Methodist, her children were baptized in her faith. She had never considered herself a religious person until her youngest son began to attend a church in

Old Fallings and invited her to join him. The church ran a playgroup and Elsie decided to work with them one morning each week.

'I had no plans to stay at home when I retired and so enjoyed working with the playgroup. When two other mature helpers and me noticed that there were a few younger children and their mothers standing around, we decided to start a Carers and Toddlers group so that we could accommodate them.

'I had only been with the playgroup for a few months when I learnt that they needed someone to take it over. I was more than happy to do it.'

In her retirement, Elsie had decided to continue to use her skills and experience, partly out of her love for children but also because she wanted to provide support for many of the young mothers in the area. Knowing the level of work that would be involved in setting up a new group, Anne Lockley, who had attended the church since it had been built thirty years before, and was one of the founders of the Carers and Toddlers group, works with Elsie.

Anne says, 'I have been involved with the playgroup for the last year but worked with Elsie to set up the Carers and Toddlers group, which has been going for four and a half years. I had only just retired and when my daughter went back to work I began to look after my granddaughter. I also wanted to get involved in the community and so the Carers and Toddlers group was perfect for me, because I could do both those things. My granddaughter was one of the first children to attend when the group started.

'We called the group Carers and Toddlers because we realized that, as well as mothers, there were fathers and grandparents looking after children and they too needed to get out and meet other people. It was also good for the children to mix with each other.'

Anne Lockley had much experience in working with children. She had brought up her own, had been a school cook, ran the local youth club and was now looking after her grandchildren. But she was still to learn a lot from Elsie.

'Elsie has what it takes to work with children. Sometimes I think she's a little strict, but the children love and respond to her, no matter what she does.

'They will be running around and she'll say, "Time for register," and they'll all stop and sit down. They are only two and half, and yet you won't hear a murmur in the room, not a movement, when the register is being called.

'She is very organized, and gets the children working on different things while they are playing. They do their numbers and have plenty of fun putting them up on the board. They know their colours, and play games with shapes. I am always amazed at how quickly they learn all the different shapes, from their rectangles to their triangles.

'Elsie believes that the children can learn while they play and they do. She's meticulous and says it's important to teach the children how to hold the pencil properly when they try to write their names. Now, I would think that that would come with time but Elsie feels they have to start off by holding the pencil right in the first place.'

Elsie encourages the children to be independent and, harking back to her own childhood, they are given little jobs. Helping to put the chairs out, to clear up at the end of the day, or to put the toys and paints away, is hardly the same as pushing a hundredweight of coke up a hill in a trolley with faulty wheels, but Elsie feels the setting of such small tasks helps to conjure up a spirit of cooperation and engenders a sense of responsibility.

Dialogue and conflict resolution also found a place in how Elsie treats some of the world's youngest citizens. They learn that it is wrong to hit other children, or to shove and push each other around. Anne explains, 'If the children upset each other, Elsie will listen to both sides, make a ruling and then get them to shake hands. It is wonderful to see how they respond.

'Only the other day she called two children to her, who were having a little squabble. The one child had left a little mark on the other child's hand. Elsie showed this to the child who had caused it, pointing out what he had done. The child not only said sorry, but put his hand on the other child's shoulder to register his feelings. That slight touch, to me, spoke volumes. So often children will say, "Sorry," because you tell them to. This child, I felt, understood why he was saying it.'

There has also been a positive response from the younger mums. Those who bring their children along feel very comfortable about leaving them with Elsie and her colleagues.

'They seem to appreciate having an older person looking after their children,' Anne says. 'They'll say, "Please look after her: she's not well today," or something and they know that you will do it. They know that you have a little more time, more experience, having brought up your own children, that you will sit them on your lap and comfort them if they need it.

'During the first few mornings they cry for their mothers and then they settle down. Often I want to pick them up and give them a cuddle but Elsie will say to leave them for a little while and then they do settle. She is often the first to say No to the children, which ties in with her idea of discipline and order. She also introduces us by our surnames and that's how the children have to address us. She is firm but very gentle with them and she likes us to be the same.

'The children also respond to you because they see you as a bit of a grandma, they see you in that light rather than a substitute mother. Sometimes when I come in and I see them running around I think, oh dear, but then when I go home I feel lively. They bring you out of yourself.'

Many of the single mothers on the estate are grateful for the start Elsie has enabled their children to have when they graduate to nursery schools.

Maxine Pinches says, 'I have three children, a boy aged eight and two girls. Samantha, who is two and a half, started the playgroup in January 2000 and Sophie, who is fifteen months, I take to the Carers and Toddlers group with me.

'Samantha attended both the groups, and as a mother I have felt that both my children have benefited a great deal.

'The Carers and Toddlers group has provided a time for me to meet other mums while Samantha plays with the other children, learns nursery rhymes, or plays numbers and alphabet games. The group has made her more confident, and she is always happy to come home with cards and paintings for me.

'The playgroup in the morning is different, because Samantha has to follow a routine and has to listen to what Elsie and the other volunteers have to say. I think this will help a great deal when she starts school. Everyone at the playgroup and the Carers and Toddlers group does a tremendous job and many other mums on the estate are very grateful for all the help and support we get personally, and we appreciate the fact that our children are able to have a good start in life.

'It also helps us young mothers to think about what we can do to help ourselves, and many of us have taken the opportunity to find part-time work, or to build up our own parenting skills through volunteering with the playgroup. Sometimes being on your own with the children can be very hard, but volunteering at the playgroup helps all of us to become much calmer and patient with our children under Elsie's influence. As well as that, we know that Elsie and all the other women will provide a listening ear if we need it.'

From the start of the Carers and Toddlers group, Elsie

was concerned to have an environment that was both happy and secure for the children. She felt that this had been achieved when the children and their parents sometimes arrived early and the children themselves were reluctant to leave. She ensured the same kind of atmosphere when she took over the playgroup.

'The playgroup runs every morning during term time and we can take up to twenty-five children; we always have a waiting-list. Children come from within walking distance. There are three of us, who are mature women, and another one will be joining us soon. We are now trying to get more of the young mums involved as volunteers, because it can sometimes get very tiring for us.'

Elsie realizes the importance of knowing children individually and developing a relationship with them.

'You can say one thing to one child and it is OK, then say the same to another child and he or she will be devastated. You have to build up a separate and more personal relationship with every child. You have to get to know everything about them. You even learn to tell the difference in the way they cry.

'Sometimes they sob because they are having a tantrum or they want attention, and in a funny way you know that they will be all right when you give them a bit of love. But it's when they sniffle quietly that you know that there is something seriously wrong, that they are distressed inside. If a child has not been crying before and then starts, you begin to wonder why. Is there something wrong at home? Is Mum having some difficulties? Is there a new baby? You make a point of asking, and so you have to develop a good relationship with Mum too.

'Trust is important, with the children and with their mums. I am never afraid to raise little points with mums if I think there is a problem, and often this has led to children receiving a little extra help, like one child who required speech therapy.

'When I was a young mum I got a lot of help and support from my family. Many young mothers and their children today don't have that support, and I feel that everything should be done to make sure that they do.'

Elsie collects her things to leave. Another day is over and the room that had held twenty-five children of all different backgrounds, playing happily together, painting or sticking colourful shapes on the walls, is now quiet. She arranges her elegant hat. Her son thought it looked out of place on a working-class estate, but Elsie said, 'If a hat is good enough for Windsor or other places, it is good enough for The Scotlands.'

When asked about the philosophy that lies behind her work, Elsie says she seeks to encourage rather than to inspire.

'You can always find the time to do what you want to do. Everybody has a role to play. The menial jobs no one wants to do are often seen as insignificant, but they are important, for they are the foundations from which bigger things can be built. As in my own experience: I was only making the tea when I first started – but someone had to do it.

'There was a time when I was someone's daughter, then I became someone's wife and later someone's mother. Now I am a person in my own right.

'My message is to go for it, girls. Remember we are all girls. We may be fifty, sixty, seventy or eighty on the outside but on the inside we are all still around twenty.'

Throughout the world, women who have sought change or to better the quality of life for people around them have often begun with educational and care facilities for small children. The adage 'The hand that rocks the cradle rules the world' seems particularly apt and, as long as there are women like Elsie Saunders helping to guide the young generations, there will always be hope that the world may become an even better place.

Miriam Long

2   A Life that Has to be Lived

Any pregnant woman's most fervent wish is that her unborn baby will emerge into the world healthy. Giving birth is still hazardous for both mother and child and a birth is usually greeted with relief as well as joy when mother and baby are pronounced fit and well. Sometimes, despite advances in antenatal care, and the most modern medical facilities, things can and do go tragically wrong.

Imagine, then, the terror and desolation of a young woman, expecting her first baby, who has a sense that there is something wrong during the very late stages of her pregnancy. Envisage her frustration as she lies helpless in a hospital bed and her pleas for assistance go unheard. What if the child develops health problems on account of this negligence? And what can ever compensate for the pain of hopes and ambitions that will remain unfulfilled for ever?

On hearing of such tragedy we can well relate to a sense of grievance, but more often than not the most common emotion is thankfulness that one has not had to suffer a comparable experience.

Miriam Long does not have to imagine. Twenty-five years ago she underwent a traumatic ordeal when her daughter Marie was born. The repercussions of that event shaped and still shape both their lives.

A slight, demure Asian woman with short black hair, Miriam arrives early at the Broadway Shopping Centre in Bexley Heath, London, and begins to put up the exhibition stands and arrange small information leaflets on long foldaway tables. It is the last day of Learning Disability Week and Miriam and her colleagues will give out contact numbers and advice to passers-by about the services available for children with difficulties.

A few people stop to take up a leaflet; one is a woman who says she thinks her three-year-old daughter has behavioural problems. Miriam responds with an understanding the woman intuitively knows has its origins in first-hand knowledge of the subject. After talking for a short while, Miriam senses that the woman has an inkling that her daughter may actually have a learning disability but prefers to believe that the child is going through a difficult phase in her development and that it will soon pass. Miriam understands that, too.

Miriam Long was born in Calcutta in 1957. Her father, Solomon Daniel, although a qualified accountant, worked as an administrator with the YMCA until 1962, when he left Calcutta for a similar post in London. Her mother, Mary Grace, was a primary-school teacher and took care of Miriam and her older brother, John, and sister, Dorothy, until they were able to travel to England a year later.

'My father had a small two-bedroom flat in Fitzroy Square near Euston. My mum and dad had one room, I shared the other with my sister, and my brother had to have one of the students' rooms. We had a bathroom but the kitchen was one that we had to share with other people who were also renting rooms.

'My mother had taught English in Calcutta, but because she didn't have a good command of spoken English she took a job as a seamstress at the YMCA, mending sheets and repairing shirt collars.'

The Daniels were devout Christians and during the year that he spent alone in England, Solomon received help and support from members of his local church. They were just as welcoming to his family when they joined him.

Work at the YMCA, where he was responsible for the accommodation and welfare of Asian students, went well until the manager, who was supposedly a family friend, requested that he worked on Sundays. Preferring to honour his family and church commitments, Solomon refused and was immediately dismissed.

'This was a difficult time for us because Mum also lost her job and we had nowhere to live. Luckily, someone from the church who worked at Harrods had managed to arrange an interview for my dad and he then got a job as a messenger.'

Now homeless, the Daniel family was in desperate straits and had little option but to take one-bedroom accommodation in a hostel which was already overcrowded with overseas students and people waiting for permanent housing.

Fortunately, within a few months life improved when Solomon's accountancy skills were recognized at Harrods and he was promoted to a job in the accounts department. They were able to find more suitable accommodation in a Victorian house that backed onto Regents Park, one of London's most picturesque and frequented localities. But the constant upheaval both at work and in trying to find a decent place for his family to live placed a heavy burden on Solomon, who had left India unprepared for these kinds of challenge.

'My dad was a very conscientious man and was always grateful for whatever opportunities came his way. His promotion at Harrods brought with it other responsibilities that he was determined to live up to. One morning he was on his way to another department when a nurse saw him slumped on the window-ledge. He had suffered a major heart attack. I was on a school trip at the time and arrived home to the news that he was in hospital.'

With the love and care of his wife Solomon Daniel recovered, and for a short time the family was sanguine once again. However, a few months later they were again uprooted without warning.

'As a family we got on well with the elderly Jewish couple who were the owners of the Victorian house we lived in, but then, out of the blue, their son came over from America, sold the house and put them into a nursing-home. We had to apply for emergency accommodation and were then moved to a house in north London that was waiting to be demolished.

'This proved too much for my dad and two years after he had his first heart attack, he suffered a second one and died.'

Solomon Daniel's dream when he got on the boat to England was to provide for his family in the best way that he could, and give them the opportunities for a better life. But within nine years of leaving his homeland he had lost the job to which he had travelled; the family he loved was reduced to a life of relative poverty which included twice being made homeless; and then he was forced to retire prematurely because of ill health. In spite of the support he received from the Church, the stress and disappointments that plagued him as he struggled in an alien land had proved too great.

Mary Grace and her children moved to a new council house in west London, and when her two oldest children were married she was left to bring up a rather rebellious Miriam.

'I missed my dad and, although I knew how difficult it was for Mum, when I was a teenager I wanted the type of freedom my friends had. They were able to go out to discos, they had boyfriends and could do what they wanted.

'I was at secondary school at the time and thought that my mum was being a snob for wanting me to go on to university when I didn't want to study. I threatened to leave home and I guess that my mum had enough when I started to dress like a hippie.

'Her response was to march me down to the cemetery where my dad was buried and she broke down and started praying to God to help her cope with me in this strange country and for the strength just to carry on. I felt ashamed and guilty about the way I had been behaving, because I loved my mum, and so I ended my rebellious period then.'

The rebellion over, during the rest of her adolescence Miriam was able to develop a more understanding and supportive relationship with her mother. It was a time when she felt confident enough to introduce her mother to a young man from the church who wanted to go out with her.

After meeting Miriam's boyfriend, Mary Grace suggested that they should get married if they intended to have a serious relationship.

Miriam was married at sixteen and became pregnant at eighteen. Her daughter Marie was born on Friday, 12 September 1974.

'I wanted my first child to have the best treatment and so I chose to give birth at a women's hospital near Hampstead where all the doctors were female. My sister had her first child there and recommended it to me. It had been the right decision for her, but it was the biggest mistake I ever made.'

During her last antenatal appointment, Miriam went into labour, with regular contractions, and was taken straight to the maternity hospital, where she remained for three days. Although the contractions continued during this time no attempt was made to examine her and it was a complete surprise to her and the rest of the family when she was discharged. Miriam was told that she had been experiencing what was known as the 'Braxton Hicks', practice contractions which were not particularly painful and considered quite normal. Her mother did not agree.

'My waters weren't breaking but it was like a drip, and so my mother called the hospital and I was taken back into hospital only a few days after I had been sent home. Still they did nothing but say that I was having contractions. I was eighteen years of age, having my first child, and I was very frightened and knew nothing about what was really happening to me. I simply trusted everybody, and when the nurse said that they would "dope me up" so that it would slow the labour down I had no idea what this meant or how it would affect me.

'An hour or so later I was given an internal examination and told that my baby was in fetal distress and that I had to have an emergency Caesarean section. Marie was born within five minutes, and looked absolutely perfect.'

However, Miriam suspected that all was not well when, within a few hours of her birth, Marie began to scream and she was unable to comfort her. Breast-feeding was proving difficult, because the newborn baby regurgitated her mother's milk. Concerned for her baby, Miriam sought help from the nursing staff but was treated with disdain.

'At first I was ignored when I tried to draw attention to the fact that my child was not feeding properly and then I was disparagingly asked if I considered myself to be the "Queen of Sheba" and told that I would know better after having six children. I was not feeling well in myself and had a wound infection, and after I was given an antibiotic injection I was told to stop being a panicky fusspot.

'In desperation I asked a paediatrician who had come to see another baby to look at my child but he refused, saying there was nothing wrong with her.'

Miriam left hospital without any special advice or acknowledgement of her concerns about her baby's health, but she felt that this would be rectified with the help of a health visitor. But no one came to visit. Feeling vulnerable, she moved in with her mother, not only for much-needed help and support but also to be close to the health clinic, which was near the council estate where her mother lived. It appeared to be the right thing to do when, within a week, the baby seemed to have settled.

'I was pleased when Marie seemed to be doing all right, although she was still vomiting after I had finished feeding her. Sometimes it was small amounts, but then it gradually increased. Mum and I took her to the clinic, and at first they said that it was because I was young and did not know how to feed her. They did not take into account that I was with my mother who, having brought up her own children, was there to help and support me. At this time Marie was not gaining weight, having been only five pounds, or just over two kilograms, at birth. The best advice from the clinic was that I should stop breast-feeding her and put her on the bottle.'

Miriam did as suggested and in desperation she tried many different types of bottles and teats in the hope that the child would feed, but it continued to be a struggle. In despair she returned to the clinic and demanded to see the doctor, suggesting that she should try feeding the child.

'Marie would not take the bottle and I remember the doctor saying how determined she was as she screamed and wriggled in her arms. Then without any explanation the doctor started to measure her head. I stood and watched, wondering why this was being done but feeling too numb and tired to ask.

'I was then instructed to take her to another hospital, still without explanation, but I did so straight away.'

Panic-stricken, although grateful for her mother's presence, Miriam fretted over what could be wrong with her baby as they travelled by bus to the hospital. After eight months, during which time the baby had refused to feed, had slept very little, cried relentlessly while Miriam and her mother took turns to stay awake to comfort her, and numerous visits to the clinic, Marie was diagnosed with hydrocephalus, excess fluid on the brain.

A devastated Miriam wept bitterly. The child's discomfort had been originally assumed to be a stomach upset and she had been given the wrong treatment; now Miriam simply did not know what to expect.

'I just couldn't understand why this had happened to us. Why had no one listened to me when I was in hospital, or when I visited the clinic? Why had they been so quick to dismiss everything I had been saying? My only hope was that there would be no long-term damage to my baby daughter.'

During the weeks that followed Miriam took her daughter back and forth to the hospital for regular scans and examinations. A month after hydrocephalus had been diagnosed Miriam was told that it was possible that her daughter would have a learning disability but that her condition could be managed. She had hardly had time to understand the implications of that when, after further examination, she was told Marie might also have a hearing problem.

'I could not believe this, particularly when Marie had been saying words like "Mum" and making the kinds of noises that all babies make. I thought that they were also able to see for themselves that she responded to the sounds of the rattle they often used when they were testing her hearing. It didn't occur to me that Marie was simply turning to follow the moving object, as opposed to responding to the sounds of the rattle.

'When Marie was nineteen months, my husband and I were asked to meet the ear, nose and throat consultant, who informed us that our daughter was profoundly deaf.

'My world shattered around me as we were forced to take in the words neither of us wanted to hear. We had been coping well with Marie, but to learn that she would have an added disability was too much for us to deal with at that time. I cried as I thought about how much our tiny baby had suffered when help should have been at hand.' It was no comfort when the consultant added, in an attempt to reassure them, that diagnosis is 'where the help starts'.

For the next few months, Miriam and her husband attended courses for families with newly diagnosed deaf children. The courses were organized to teach parents how to communicate and look after their children and about the various gesturing techniques to which their children were most likely to respond. They were also made aware of the tension that can arise within families which include a child with a disability, and of the high percentage of family breakdown when that tension proves too great to bear. Miriam, aged nineteen, had entered a world she could not have imagined.

'I had no doubts that I would have to do everything I could to make Marie's life as fulfilled as possible. Communication was going to be the biggest challenge and we were taught how important it was to make sure that the child would look and be on a level where she could see your own face.

'Marie was issued with hearing aids that were far too big for her because she was so tiny, and I was taught how to look after them. As a parent with a newly diagnosed child, I felt safe in the knowledge that I had support, even though when I left the training-course I had to face the reality alone.'

The next two years were demanding ones which saw Miriam spending most of her time with her daughter at home and at a nursery school for deaf children. Although the children had varying levels of deafness, they could communicate and were able to grasp the sign language that little Marie could not.

With great sadness, Miriam had to accept that her daughter would not be joining the other children, who were able to progress to other classes. 'We always knew that educating Marie was going to be a problem. Being profoundly deaf and having a learning disability meant that she needed to be in an environment where she could have total communication, and we asked for a diagnosis that would confirm that.

'My second daughter, Elisabeth, was born when Marie was five years old. It was hard at first to cope with both children, because Marie was not progressing, and once again my mother was my main support.

'We wanted the best for Marie and took a while to find the right school for her. At the age of six, we thought we had found the right place at a boarding-school in Buckinghamshire which would provide the total care she needed. It was weekly boarding, and that meant Marie was able to come home at weekends.'

For the first two weeks Marie seemed to have settled, but without warning she became distressed and the school found it difficult to cope with her.

'I still don't know just how we got through that period, which was very painful for us. Marie would come home with bruises all over her because she just thrashed about and was very aggressive. This was made worse by the fact that she was having difficulty sleeping and would start wandering about during the night. We knew she was capable of this, because she had been like that at home.

'We talked with the school and it was then realized that what she needed was more of the one-to-one support she had been used to at home.'

In order to give Marie the educational support she needed, Miriam had joined an organization for children with special needs and started a programme designed to provide the extra stimulation Marie required.

Each week Marie was expected to achieve a simple task, like brushing a doll's hair, but more importantly she was encouraged to learn how to match pictures with words, a task which was to affect every aspect of the Longs' household.

'Every item in our house was labelled – chairs, tables, hall, carpet, stairs, in fact everything you could possibly think of. She knew all these words by the time she started boarding-school but they didn't have programmes like this.

'I was always with her and had encouraged her to do things for herself and rewarded her often with a hug or a kiss because I wanted her to know how much we loved her. She could use the toilet by herself but she would not always remember to wash her hands, and so I was always reminding her and she would run up the stairs and do it and return with a wide grin because she knew that she had achieved something.

'When we talked with the school about this they were wonderful and assigned her someone who would spend more time with her.'

Marie improved and was progressing in every way. It was a great joy when she had managed to learn around ninety signs, and there was a flicker of hope that she would at long last have a means of communication.

It was clear that her relationship with her teacher was good and that she had managed to learn many new things and was much more controlled. Miriam was delighted with her daughter's progress and felt that she could not have asked for more.

'For the first time in years we saw a marked improvement. And then her teacher left and there was no one to take over what he had been able to provide. Once again we thought that we had overcome another barrier only to be disappointed. It was also clear to us that Marie needed some consistency in her life. Unfortunately, this had been taken away and she began to regress.'

The situation for Marie did not improve but she was able to remain at the boarding-school until she was thirteen years old. Then the teachers felt they could no longer meet her needs and suggested that she went to another school in Manchester.

She was offered a place at a school for deaf children. It was set in excellent grounds, employed hearing specialists, psychologists and had a medical centre. Marie remained there for six years, but her progress was not what Miriam had hoped for or expected.

When Marie was nineteen Miriam received a letter from the social services informing her that they would no longer provide finances for any further educational support Marie required. The letter added that the funding for Marie's college place was to cease forthwith.

'I just went mad at this unexpected bombshell. What could I do with a nineteen-year-old who had no speech, a limited amount of sign language and still required plenty of support?

'They had started a transition assessment when she was sixteen, but when the community nurse left she was not replaced and no one else continued the assessment. In spite of our requests they did nothing. If this assessment had been done properly, Marie would have had options as an individual.

'Instead, they offered to send her to a centre for people with profound and complex needs, and I said, "No way." I had heard of the place and knew that it would not have suited Marie. It was mostly for people who could do very little for themselves and had to be fed or taken to the toilet – in fact, everything had to be done for them. Marie could do things for herself but needed support; a place like that would simply have seen her regress even further.

'There seemed no let-up in finding what was right for our daughter, and at that time I was admitted to hospital for an operation and we had little choice but to allow her to go to a place we knew would not be good for her, because there was nowhere else for her.

'As soon as I came out of hospital, I got her out of there. I had found a course at a local college that was for people with learning difficulties and wanted my daughter to go there, knowing that this was a more appropriate place for her, as long as she could have some support.'

From the day Marie was born, Miriam knew that her life was sure to be very different from the one she had hoped and planned for. She had fought many personal and public battles to secure the best for her child, and had started a self-advocacy group for people with a learning disability, to help to highlight what is needed to improve the services they require.

Her fight to continue Marie's educational support involved meetings with many different agencies, heads of departments, her local councillors, care and welfare officers. Miriam's small living-room was often packed with people who could appreciate that, although Marie was a young woman with complex needs, it was unfair to assign her to a place that would encroach on the quality of life she deserved.

'The support we had was phenomenal and I was given words of encouragement by many people. It made me realize how easy it is for a member of a minority group, especially someone who hasn't got a voice, to be forgotten. I felt strongly that even people with complex needs should be given a choice; that, no matter how disabled they are in terms of their physicality or the environment, they should be able to make choices in their own lives. Even a child can make this choice by crying when they need their mother or someone else. My daughter and others like her are adults and should be treated as such.

'I believe that there is a lack of respect everywhere for people who have a learning or physical disability. You see it when you visit some day centres. Staff point at people and they say things like "You behave yourself"; it is a kind of attitude that is insensitive and degrading. It is very sad, because people with learning and physical disabilities have to trust the people who are there to help them. They are often conditioned to think that they are being treated in the proper way, but very often they are not. People who are in the system may not see this, but going in from the outside a person can see it in a different light.'

Miriam appealed against the decision of the social services and won her case. This meant Marie started the year-long college course in September 1994 and was given a support worker. Miriam later learnt that the department's reluctance to support her daughter had its origins in their belief that they would be setting a precedent. They argued that, because so many young people had a learning disability, they could not be seen to be supporting one person but not others.

'I had read the Community Care Act and knew that the department had a responsibility to meet the person's individual needs and not focus on their own financial situation. All this fighting wore me out, but I knew that I simply had to keep going.'

Miriam's focus on meeting her daughter's needs brought conflict into other aspects of her family life. There had been times of great sorrow and pain, including the end of her marriage. But it was the death of her mother, without whose support she probably would not have had the strength to endure, that was the hardest for her to cope with.

Living alone after all her children had married and moved away, Mary Grace Daniel had eventually moved into sheltered accommodation to be near her daughter. After having her third child, Jonathan, Miriam wanted to return to a course of study and her mother took great pleasure in looking after her grandson.

'My mum was the person I most looked up to. She was my rock and I simply could not have coped without her. She came to see me one afternoon and said that she was going into hospital for a minor operation and that I wasn't to worry about anything. In fact, she had cancer and had to have a mastectomy. The cancer had spread and because of her age the hospital decided that they would not provide any further treatment.'

Mary Grace did not inform her children of the seriousness of her condition but chose instead to visit some of the places she had always wanted to see. She travelled to Greece, Israel and Cyprus before spending time with relatives in Canada. On her return, though, her condition deteriorated.

'The week before Mum died she called us, the family and some of her closest friends, together for a meal in her sheltered accommodation and then on the Tuesday she had a hospital appointment and I went with her. I couldn't stay because I needed to get back for the girls, who were coming home for lunch, and Mum had asked if I could not have let them stay at school for lunch so that I could stay with her. It was the first time she had made any demands on me. For my mum, it had always been give, give, give. I just didn't realize that she was that ill and was in fact very frightened.

'On the Thursday of that week, I got a call from the warden saying my mum had taken ill and that an ambulance had come. I raced to the flat and then followed the ambulance to the hospital, still thinking that she would get better and come home. By the evening my mum was in such pain that the doctors had to administer diamorphine. We were all by her bedside when she died on Saturday morning, apart from my sister, who had stayed with Mum throughout the night and had just gone home for a rest.'

None of the family coped very well with Mary Grace's death. For them the very foundation of their lives had been taken away. A few years later, Miriam and her husband divorced, as did her brother and his wife.

'It was as though it was Mum that was holding all of us together. No matter the difficulties in our personal lives, we told Mum nothing about them because we knew how much they would have troubled her. She had been at the centre of our lives. After her death, we all had to accept that there was an emptiness in our lives which only Mum could have filled. Nothing and no one else could replace her.'

For a moment, Miriam reflects upon the woman whom she revered as a role model as well as a mother.

'My mother had always instilled in us that we were always to find work, no matter what it was, and so I always worked. I had done child-minding and stacked shelves before working with social services. It was a culture I was used to and, with Mum now gone, I had to rely on myself to continue to provide for my children and to fight for Marie. She had at least left me with the strength and courage to do that.'

But Miriam was able, in part, to fill the void in her life through her voluntary work with the National Deaf Children's Society. Despite taking care of Marie and her three other children, she found the time to establish a youth club for deaf children and their families with funding she received from the Scarman Trust. The group meets every Wednesday for over two hours at the Dresdner Kleinwort Benson Sports Ground in New Eltham, London. The children are involved in sport, music, using computers and other activities.

'I started the club because I felt that, while there were things for children with a learning disability, there was nothing for deaf children in my area. I would have welcomed such an activity myself when Marie was small. I also felt that it was important for the children not to feel isolated, and I encouraged their brothers and sisters also to attend as well as their parents.'

In spite of the interest in the club, when it first started only two or three children turned up with their parents. But Miriam continued to promote it, taking heart from the fact that the children who did attend wanted to come and benefited from the activities. Realizing that transport was a problem, she hired a minibus and recruited drivers. The club is now thriving, with up to twelve young people between the ages of eleven and twenty, and their siblings, attending at any one time.

Miriam's work was brought to the attention of a company called Britannia Software, which chooses an organization to sponsor each year. The staff were pleased not only to donate equipment and to help with publicizing the group, but also to attend the sessions and to gain a better awareness of the needs of deaf children.

Mark Johnson, the member of staff who worked with Miriam, speaks of the benefits. 'Each year our company is dedicated to one charity and Miriam's name was put forward. Miriam had done quite a lot of work herself and we were very impressed with just what she had achieved. I went along to the club and brought my family with me, as I felt that it was important for all of us to understand that it is possible to communicate with deaf children; but, more importantly, that although they have special needs these children are still capable of achieving many things. I felt that it was good that the children were being integrated so that barriers could be broken down. There was nothing like this youth club in the area and we were pleased to have the opportunity to support Miriam and her project.'

Marie is now twenty-five and living at home with her mother, sisters Elisabeth and Joanna, her younger brother, Jonathan, and baby niece, Bethany. Miriam is fighting for her to have assisted independent living accommodation.

Miriam's second daughter, Elisabeth, admires her mother's courage and determination and has given her support over the years.

'My mother is a very determined woman in her work and in everything else she does. It is very important to her to carry on going, even if it doesn't seem like she is getting anywhere. She just tries to juggle everything, even now when she is fighting for Marie's independence.

'I sometimes wish that I could have more time with her or that she could spend more time with us, but there is always something she has to do. I know that many families have benefited from the youth club but sometimes I think she takes on too much, particularly when people are phoning up all the time.

'She does what she does because of Marie, but she has also managed to give us all the love and support that we needed when we were children. I don't feel that I have missed out. She's very caring and committed to what she does. I am glad that she is my mother.'

Miriam smiles as she hears Elisabeth's words, but the eyes that mirror her daughter's love also betray regrets. The greatest of them is that she cannot communicate in that way with her eldest daughter and that she is not able to enter Marie's silent world.

'Looking back, I probably would not have had my first child so young and I wish that I had not had Marie at that hospital. They did not monitor me. Nowadays you are monitored but in those times there were no scans, no ultrasound. I had one X-ray when I was six months pregnant and they said that, because I was small, there might be problems with the birth. So why did they leave it until Marie was in distress? She might still have had some problems but they might not have been so severe.

'When I had my other children, my consultant didn't even contemplate letting me have a natural birth and so I had elective Caesarean sections for them.

'Many people have asked why my husband and I did not bring a case against the hospital, but when we tried to get the birth notes it was claimed that they had been lost. In any case, we could not have coped with taking up a case. When you have a child with complex needs, your life revolves around that. Coping with everyday life is enough. Taking a court case would have been too much. I don't regret not having sued the hospital, because Marie lives. She has her own finances, through the Independent Living Fund, which she needs for everyday life. What good would money do that it is not doing already?

'She has a life, and it is a life that has to be lived.'

Maria Kwawang

3   *The River is My Friend*

At 6.30 on a spring Sunday morning in Handsworth the air is fresh and crisp. Maria Kwawang, a tall, elegant black woman, stands at a bus stop in one of Birmingham's most notorious inner-city areas. She pulls the collar of her coat up around her ears, and pushes her hands deep into her pockets to shield them from the cold. Two other people who are making their way slowly along the grey pavements, made treacherous by the glistening morning frost, join her.

Minutes later the bus arrives and Maria shows her pass to the driver as she boards. In a sparsely filled vehicle, she settles in a seat by the window to begin the half-hour journey to the nursing-home, one of the two jobs she does in her efforts to provide adequately for her family.

Her life as a political refugee does not arise from personal choice but is a consequence of the devastating and bloody civil war that has raged in her country, Sudan, for over thirty years.

Maria was born in 1959, the eldest of four girls, near Malaka, a village which sits between the White Nile and the River Sobat, a hundred and seventy-five miles east of the Ethiopian border and over four hundred miles south of Khartoum. Her father was a farmer and a descendant of the royal family of the tribe of Trulouch. He died of meningitis when Maria was a young child, so she lived with her mother, uncle and sisters, one of whom died of the same disease when only four.

'My village was like a city and we lived in a villa which

51

had a thatched roof made from branches and mud. There were large rooms to accommodate our extended families. All the villas were grouped together and surrounded by a wall woven from grass.

'The climate is very hot and dry until the rainy season, which starts in April or May and continues into September. During that time you could only travel by steamer because the roads were often flooded and dangerous.

'The population was dense and a lot of villages were scattered around. My village is on an island between two rivers.

'Like most of the women in the village, my mother did the cooking, fetched water from the river and got the firewood, while my uncle, like other men, took care of the house and the harvest and went fishing. If you were a woman living in the city, you had a choice of going to work while a relative looked after your children. Women in the villages rarely had that choice.

'Most of my childhood memories are painful ones because of the civil war.'

Sudan's ongoing civil war has its origins in ancient times when the country was an arena for sometimes violent interaction between the cultures of Africa and the Mediterranean. The modern context was set in a colonial period when the country was ruled by Britain and Egypt from 1899, and northern and southern Sudan were administered separately. At independence in 1956 the Arabic north and the mostly African south became united under a government ruled from the northern city of Khartoum.

While the new government sought to control a unified Sudan, most southern Sudanese were striving for self-determination in the form of either autonomy or independence from the north. Civil war erupted when the government further tried to impose the Arabic language and the religion of Islam on the southerners, who were mainly Christian. The fact that both sides wanted to control the resources of the south – its oilfields, the Nile waters, fishing sites and grazing land – served to intensify hostilities.

'As a child I was always afraid, because when the government heard that guerrillas had passed through our villages they would send soldiers in to interrogate us. These soldiers often killed civilians and burnt their houses.

'My aunt, who I stayed with for a short time, was killed in this way. She was ill and could not run away when they came, and so they set her house alight and then threw her onto the fire. I would have been killed, too, if I had been with her.'

During the troops' incursions, the women often risked their lives by helping the village men and providing them with food. 'I remember when my mother and other women in the village would cook early so that the men and boys could eat and then go and hide before it was dark. They did this because sometimes the soldiers would come at night and look for any boy or man who was in the house. If they found them, they would be taken away and never seen alive again. Only sometimes, their bodies would be found floating in the river.

'I first saw these terrible things from the age of nine, and the images will stay with me for ever.'

As a young woman growing up in the village, Maria looked forward to times spent with friends from nearby villages.

'Back home we didn't have boyfriends and girlfriends. A group of boys would come from other villages and we would go around together for a few days. We would eat, drink soft drinks, because alcohol wasn't allowed, dance, and talk well into the night. Everything was done in the open.'

This was an acceptable form of socializing for young people in the villages, where there were heavy penalties for young women who got pregnant outside marriage.

'It would be a miserable life. Your pregnancy would be made public and you would be left with no pride or dignity in yourself. Your family, who would be embarrassed and made to feel ashamed by almost everyone in the village, would just get rid of you by marrying you off to anybody who came along. You would be treated as second-hand and would have no choice in the matter. The marriage would take place in a register office and there would be no celebration.'

Maria met her husband, Kunijwok Gwado Ayoker Kwawang, also known as Walter, during one of these gatherings. Walter's parents already knew of Maria because of dealings with her father, and were happy that their son had asked for her hand in marriage.

They eagerly negotiated their contributions with Maria's mother and her uncle, to enable the marriage to take place.

'To get married, the man's family had to give something to the woman's family. How much was given depended on the size of the man's family and how well they could match what the woman's family had. My family was quite wealthy and so Walter's family had to give cows, sheep, goats and money. It is not a dowry, but more to do with the responsibility of your husband's family to care for you. If the marriage doesn't work out and you have no children, you have to give it all back.'

It is customary for a woman to keep her maiden name but for children to take their father's name and, as well as looking after her husband, the woman looks after his family. But her family remains responsible for her welfare.

'A woman belongs to her own family and they have the right to say what she should or should not do in her marriage. A husband cannot just abandon his wife or divorce her. If anything, he has to take her back to her family.'

Maria was nineteen when she and Walter were married. Two years later, through the British Council of Churches,

Walter won a scholarship to Manchester University to study for a master's degree in anthropology. In 1978, Maria was able to join him for the first time in the country she was to escape to ten years later.

The journey to England took its toll on a young African woman who was travelling alone and outside her small village for the first time.

'I travelled on Sudan Airlines and we stopped in Cairo. There they announced instructions about where you had to go, in English and Arabic. We then stopped off in Rome, where they spoke only Arabic. By the time I got to Heathrow, the announcements were only in English and I couldn't understand a word. I felt lost and confused.

'When the security people were checking my passport, I could only nod and answer "Hmm", to everything they said. My mind went completely blank and I was very frightened. Then I met Walter and he was talking to me in my own language, but I still couldn't make out what he was saying. I just kept looking at him as if he was a stranger. When we got home to Manchester, he took me straight to the hospital but I then had to be moved to the Immigration Hospital, where they kept me for three days. I never spoke to anyone in all those days and could only think about my family at home and my son, who I had to leave behind and was just a baby. It was very hard for me to understand what was happening to me and why I was in such a state. I sat for hours just watching people around me. I never thought that I would recover.

'I had some medication and the doctor discharged me, saying that I had experienced culture shock and that I would be all right.'

The first few weeks in the small bedsit that Maria shared with Walter did not help her situation. Unable to speak English, and without friends or support, Maria became more and more isolated and depressed.

'Walter, who tried very hard to help me, said he would

pay for me to have lessons in English. He thought that if I could at least speak a little English I would not feel so alone.

'At that time I was feeling very weak and I convinced myself that I would never be able to learn the language. I told him that he would only be wasting the little money he had paying for me to learn English.'

But Walter did not give up his idea. An ambitious and educated man, he had wasted no time in teaching his wife how to read and write when they got married. The Sudanese government had no plans to provide education in the south after 1962. Once it had failed to bring the schools under Arabic influence, it brought a halt to most of the Christian missionaries' activities, which led to the closure of most of the schools in the villages and left many people like Maria without any formal education. As a means of rectifying this, it later became customary for the educated partner in a marriage to teach the other partner how to read and write. After providing Maria with these skills Walter had little doubt that he could also teach her English.

'Every afternoon when Walter came home from university, he taught me English for two hours. We would then go to the local pub, because he thought this was a place where everyone talked freely and where I would learn a lot. He would buy me an orange juice and I would sit for two hours, sometimes with his friends and sometimes on my own, just listening to people talking.

'We did this for the whole ten months that I was there, and I did learn a few words and phrases.'

Maria's understanding of English improved but she was less confident in holding conversations. After six months, during which time Walter did the shopping with her, he thought it was time for Maria to venture out on her own.

'Walter gave me some money and said I had to go and do the shopping. I would only buy the things that I could recognize in the plastic covering, like rice, or milk in a bottle.

'I wanted a tin of salmon and asked the shopkeeper to help me, but he was a grumpy man and said that I should be able to read the label myself because I had been to his shop enough times to know what I needed. Well, I could make out the word "salmon" but there were other words with it that I couldn't understand. I became very nervous because Walter had told me not to buy the salmon in shrimp sauce because neither of us liked shrimps.

'In the end I just picked up a can and the other stuff and handed over the money. I just hoped that I had enough money and when I got back some change I presumed that it was correct because I couldn't really tell.

'I was pleased with the things I had managed to buy, until Walter told me that I had actually bought the salmon with shrimps. I became very upset and angry and took the tin back to the shop. I left it on the counter and didn't even ask for my money back.'

Pregnant again, Maria returned home to Sudan to have their second child while Walter moved to Oxford University to continue his studies.

Maria was glad to be back home, but was discouraged from speaking the little English she had painstakingly managed to learn.

'People frowned when I said I could speak some English and accused me of trying to be white. Some people also said, "This is not England," and so I had to revert to speaking Schulluck, which is my tribal language, or Arabic. It wasn't long before I had forgotten all the English I had spent ten months learning.'

During Walter's period of study, Maria was able to make short visits to Britain, but found them unsettling. The time they managed to spend together amounted to around two years during the five years that Walter spent in England. By then Maria had three children and was finding it hard to cope with her children alone while also caring for Walter's family.

In 1983 Walter returned to Sudan and worked as a lecturer in politics at the University of Khartoum, before securing a position in government as minister of labour.

At last Maria felt settled with her husband and children. But the conflict in the south was re-emerging and the growing unrest elsewhere in the country, exacerbated by famine and the influx of tens of thousands of refugees from neighbouring countries, led to the government being overthrown in a bloodless coup in April 1985. The situation became dangerous for Walter because of his political activities.

'My husband was told that he was on a list of people to be arrested and that it would be better for him to leave the country. We talked about the situation and Walter suggested that I should leave with the children. I had five children by this time and my youngest was only two years old. I thought it was better for him to leave first, because of the danger, and told him that I would find a way to join him later. I thought this was better, because if we left first it would arouse suspicion and make it more difficult for him to leave.

'In any case, what could I do in England without him?'

Through the University of Khartoum, Walter hurriedly secured a sabbatical as a visiting fellow at the Selly Oak Colleges in Birmingham, and he left Sudan. Not long afterwards, a number of his colleagues were captured by the military police, tortured and imprisoned. The police searched vigorously for Walter and began to question Maria about his whereabouts. The mental anguish this situation caused was profound, but Maria knew what she had to do.

'Initially, the military police would come every week to question me. They would ask the same question, "Where is your husband?"and I would give them the same answer,

"I don't know." Then they threatened to throw me in prison and take my children away.

'Then their visits became less frequent, and in a way it was worse not knowing when they would come. Each time they came I feared that something terrible was going to happen to the children and me, but I kept calm and did not show my fear, although sometimes I knew they could see I was shaking. I worried that the day would come when they would carry out their threats, and so kept on with my plans to leave with my children.

'Then one day I went to the bank and found that they had frozen our joint bank account and I couldn't get money for the children. I asked what was going on and the manager said that he had been told by the vice-counsellor in the new government not to release any monies from that account.'

The military police thought that, without access to what was a substantial sum, Walter was sure to surface, particularly as lack of money would affect his whole family. But Maria was one step ahead of them.

'Walter and I had to look after all our relatives as well as our five children, and so I decided that I would get a job in an office or at our local hospital, but the pay wasn't very much. I then decided that I would start my own business.

'I got a licence which enabled me to travel to Kenya to buy clothes, bags, creams and perfumes. I opened a little shop in Bari and I also sold these goods on the outside markets. My mother, who had run her own business making and selling alcohol, helped me.

'I made a lot of money because rich African men would spend hundreds of [Sudanese] pounds on clothes and perfumes for their wives. Within two years I had bought three cars and three houses, and shared it all between my family and my husband's family. We had achieved a high standard of living. I also kept money in other accounts that was in my own name, Awang, and this I was able to use without the knowledge of the military police.'

Maria was able to maintain some contact with Walter through his family and friends in London, and she provided him with details of her route out of Sudan. She decided to fly from Khartoum to the Soviet Union, and then to London. If that failed, she would go to Egypt and fly to London from there.

'It took me ten months to plan everything. I first had to pay three thousand Sudanese pounds to purchase visas for the children and me, and the tickets costs one million Sudanese pounds. I bought everything in my own name and told the people at the British Embassy, where I had to get the visas, that I was going on a family holiday, and gave them the date of my return.'

Currency regulations were strict and she was permitted to take out of the country only £S22 per person. Everything else she had to leave behind.

'I had to make sure that all my family were secure in the houses we had. I sold the three cars, the jewellery and the furniture to settle all outstanding bills on some of the houses and to leave my husband's family with enough money to keep them going for a while. I left the business to my sister and brother-in-law.

'No one knew that I was leaving. I only told my mother half an hour before the taxi was due to arrive. I simply said, "Mum, I am going," and told her to sort things out after I had gone. That was it. She cried and was upset that I had not said anything before, but if I had she would have told other people and word would have probably got back to the military police. I couldn't take that risk.

'The children were all very good, and as we piled into the taxi I kept looking over my shoulder, hoping and praying that the military police would not suddenly appear.

'My heart was very heavy, but I could not allow myself

to cry. I had not said goodbye to the people I loved, and as my mother waved to me from the doorway I had a feeling that I was never going to see her again. It was a very sad day for me.'

Maria arrived safely with her children at London's Heathrow airport, where a tearful Walter met and hugged them. For Maria, it was a mixture of joy, anger, sadness and relief that she had made it. Preparing to leave Sudan had left her with little time to think of what life would be like in exile. All she knew was that there would be no more threats of torture, she would be with her husband, and her children would be safe.

It is well documented that those fleeing persecution often arrive in the country in which they are seeking refuge traumatized and psychologically ill prepared for what lies ahead of them. Maria was no different in this regard; she had had little time to settle in England when the reality of life as a refugee in a foreign country began to take its toll.

'It was a nightmare at first, but Walter was very good at sorting out everything that we needed and we both applied for political asylum. It was all very new to me and I wasn't sure what I should do. We initially got help from his friends from the British Council of Churches and we were able to find temporary accommodation on a local college campus. Walter organized the school places for our children.

'My two eldest children, Aban, fourteen and Nyathesis, who was ten, went to special classes where they learnt English, while Donny, eight, and Opiny, who was five, just had to learn the best they could in their ordinary classes. My youngest, Nyapinyotarro, was only three years old. 'Within a month we had moved to a two-bedroom Victorian house on the outskirts of Birmingham. It was very old and needed a lot of repair. The damp was terrible. You could lie down at night and feel the bedding was wet and the mould would grow on the windows. My children became very sick, and it wasn't long before I found myself thinking that I would have been better off dying in Sudan.'

Maria's despondency was compounded by the knowledge that, unlike on her previous visits when she had been
able to plan her return home, now this was no longer a
choice. Now she had to adapt to a new way of life, one
without the love and support to which she had been accustomed. In her new life in England, she saw herself as a
mere outsider, a person who could only observe the hordes
of people who passed by her new home while going about
their lives. To Maria they seemed to have a purpose that
was lacking in her own life.

'Sometimes the loneliness I felt was unbearable. It was
like I was in my own little world. I could be among people
and yet no one would see me. It was terrible. I had in my
mind things that I wanted to say, but I could not express
them.'

When Maria had been planning to join her husband in
exile, she knew it would not be easy and that it would take
time for her to come to terms with her new life. It is with
some irony that she reflects that she fled a land which had
welcomed and taken in hundreds of thousands of refugees
during the seventies and eighties. Her own position was
very different from that of those refugees. She was about to
become a member of one of the most reviled groups of
people in Western Europe: a political refugee, an asylum-
seeker. Being of a different colour in a foreign country and
unable to speak the language was, she realized, one of the
worst things that could have happened to her.

'You have no idea what people are saying about you.
They could be insulting or praising you, trying to help or
abuse you, you just don't know. But you know that they are
judging you.

'You are black, you are a foreigner, a refugee; you have
come to invade their country, to take their houses and to
take their jobs. Most people do not really know what is
happening in the world or the country from which you

have escaped. It is this ignorance that is most hurtful and damaging.

'They never stop to consider or ask why a person would leave their home or risk their life to come to a foreign country where they know that life will be a struggle. And you cannot tell them.'

Once again Maria knew that she had to overcome the language barrier and, with three other Sudanese women who had joined their husbands in exile, she started to attend English classes at her local college.

'It was a matter of survival. I had to learn to speak English, otherwise I knew that I could not succeed. If I failed, I decided that I would leave the children with Walter and go back home to face whatever was going to happen to me.'

Within two years she had a good command of English, had found a job in a residential nursing-home and had formed the Sudanese Women's Group. Members of the group began to meet in one another's homes for moral support and to make sense of the new culture.

'Back home in our villages, it was not possible for a person to feel alone. There was always someone to help, support and guide you. In England it was so different. You never knew where you were with people. One day I would say hello and people would respond. Other times when I said hello, the same people would turn away. I really couldn't understand this.

'In our group we were from different tribes but we could all speak Arabic. We drew strength from our experiences from home, which we knew was going to make life a little easier for us in our new environment.'

Maria's fighting spirit returned and she took up the challenge to seek better accommodation.

'We lived – five children and two adults – in that two-bedroom Victorian house for four years, simply because I did not have the language or the courage to tell anyone about the poor conditions. Walter was mostly in London trying to find work so I knew it was up to me to do something about it.

'At first I went to the housing office and they said I didn't have enough points, which were awarded each year, to justify a move. I needed three hundred, and realized that by the time I got those points my children would all have probably grown up and left home.

'I went to the Citizens' Advice Bureau [CAB], but they could not help. My last stop was to go the Refugee Council, and I threatened to leave my husband and my children if something was not done.'

Within two months Maria and her family were offered a larger house, though this one, too, needed repair.

'Damp was once again a problem, the roof was leaking and the plaster was peeling off the walls. We tried to argue for improvement, but were told that we were lucky to have been offered a property. The housing office kept promising to send someone in to repair the roof, but we had to wait for months.

'I did the best that I could to make the house a home, but I kept feeling sick and had headaches. I thought there was something wrong with the gas fire we had in the front room and mentioned this to Walter. He said it was all in my imagination and that I was thinking too much about our problems.

'One day when he was away I decided to call the gas emergency service. They came and found that the chimney was blocked and said that we were lucky to be alive.'

Drawing on her own experiences, Maria began to encourage other women in the group to voice their needs and concerns. Many were also having problems with poor housing and were under pressure to find work, even though they were unable to speak English or to understand what was expected of them. Her English had improved to such an extent that it enabled her to accompany and interpret for those who still found it difficult to express themselves. She also provided personal support and encouragement wherever it was needed.

Grace Gordon Abiye Makvac is quick to recount how she benefited from that support.

'I remember when I first met Maria. She had arrived a few months before me and so was able to help me to settle in.

'My father was a lawyer in Sudan and I grew up in Khartoum. I didn't really have the type of practical skills of someone like Maria, who lived in the village, and found it hard to adapt.

'I was very depressed and cried a lot because I felt so isolated. The weather didn't help: it was always cold or raining. The fact that I couldn't speak English made matters worse.

'At one time I wanted to kill myself because I couldn't see a way out of my situation. I began to neglect myself and started to overeat. I wanted to look ugly. My husband was very upset with me and my baby daughter seemed always to be crying.

'Maria started to talk with me, and said I wasn't to give up hope. I had only one child and she had five. She was a little older than me and so I listened and felt comforted by her. She helped me to believe in myself and then she encouraged me to go with her to college to learn English.

'I always enjoyed studying and went on to do a number of other courses after I reached a good standard in English. I am now looking to run my own small catering business.

'At the time when I was at my lowest, Maria was there to help me learn to help myself.'

But no one was there to help Maria, who had many barriers to overcome as her own problems seemed to multiply day by day.

She had to make regular trips to the housing office because the house remained in need of repair. She encountered many problems when claiming benefits for her children. And she had to cope with her two eldest children, who had both left school and could not find work.

Walter, too, was without work, and as the sole bread-winner Maria had found a job at another residential home. She worked early, late and night shifts. One job often ran into the other, sometimes with only a five-hour break in between. At such times, when she became weary, she thought of her family at home and the life of luxury that she had left behind.

'I would have good days and very bad days. There seemed no place to go with the problems I had, and when the bills began to pile up I just couldn't cope.

'Eventually I went to the Citizens' Advice Bureau. The person I saw was very sympathetic and called the benefits office straight away. After her conversation with them she assured me that everything would be OK.

'When I went to the benefits office, the person who had been dealing with my case and had spoken with the woman at CAB had gone off sick, and I had to speak with someone else. This other person asked me the same questions that had already been answered by the woman at the CAB so I was back to square one.'

This vicious and frustrating circle went on for years. But there was some comfort for the family when they were moved to better accommodation.

More settled in her new home, and attuned to the arduous working hours, Maria's spirits rose again. Not only were her new neighbours welcoming but on occasion they took her children to school when her shift made it difficult for her to do so. She often returned the favour.

'One particular morning, when I collected my neighbour's six-year-old son, he was surprised to see me in my tribal dress. I was wearing a colourful wrap which was tied across my shoulders and is called a *"lou"*, and a headpiece that matched. It was the first time in almost three years that I had worn that outfit.

'He asked why I was dressed like that and I said because it made me feel like I was at home. He then said, "But this is not your home, and you shouldn't dress in that way."

'I didn't mind his comments because I understood that, for a child, seeing me in a dress that was so different to what he thought was normal was sure to create a reaction. But what happened later that morning was unforgivable.'

Having taken the children to school, Maria decided to go into the city centre to do the weekly shopping. She had just stepped onto the escalator in the Bull Ring, the main shopping centre in Birmingham, when she heard loud voices shouting for someone to stop. Maria did not respond, as she thought that the shouts could not have been directed at her.

As she reached the top of the escalator, two policemen suddenly jostled her and moved her briskly into a shop doorway. Shaken and confused, Maria became anxious.

'One of the policemen, who was standing very close to me, said he had a few questions to ask me because I fitted the description of someone they were looking for. I explained my situation, but I could see from their faces that they did not believe me. I asked them where the description came from and they said Henworth.

'I was amazed. I had only just managed to find my way around one small part of the large city of Birmingham, and had never even heard of Henworth. They asked me about the way I was dressed and then told me that I looked very strange. I did not respond to this because I didn't know how to. Instead, I asked them what was the crime. They said they could not tell me and then asked me for some identification. I gave them my green pass, which had my name, address and photograph on it.

'As they were looking at the card, I told them that I didn't believe that there was a crime but that wearing my own traditional clothes had made me a criminal in Birmingham.

'They gave me back my pass and walked away without an apology. I was left feeling humiliated and deeply hurt. A few people who had gathered to look on at what was happening began to walk away, and I had a sinking and hollow feeling inside me. I was too upset to do my shopping, and so got on a bus and went home.'

This was the first of many experiences which made Maria acutely aware of her difficult status and compounded her sense of unbelonging.

It was a coincidence that the very group that she had started became her main source of support.

Within four years the Sudanese Refugee Community in Birmingham had grown from five to twenty families and with that came further demands on Maria, who by then had emerged as a leader in her community.

'We became a very mixed group. Some people could speak English, some could not. Some had found work while others were still looking, under the constant pressure of losing their benefits. Most of the men were overqualified and simply could not find work, while our children were behind with their school work because of language difficulties.'

Maria expanded the group to cater for the various needs and interests of individuals when their social isolation and difficulties began to affect their self-esteem and mental health.

'In the majority of cases it was left to the women to hold families together and to support the children. Men were either despairing because they couldn't find a job or else turning to alcohol as a means of escaping from all the problems.

'There were many traditional skills among the women: working with beads, weaving, hair-plaiting, and needlework, including embroidery and crocheting and working with textiles. We decided to use these skills to set up small community enterprises. We also began planning a Women's Centre, where these enterprises could be developed; it would also act as a meeting-place for us, outside our homes, where we could hold discussions and social gatherings.

'We felt it was important to preserve the language of our children and to teach them about their history so that they could understand why we had to leave our country. We decided that we would do this through various sessions and links with a Saturday school that had been set up by the Refugee Council.'

Within a few months, Maria was able to raise funds for sewing-machines, material and other equipment, and the group found a room at their local community centre and began to develop their ideas.

All the women had left behind them the years of painful isolation. They had rediscovered the eagerness and tenacity that had been lost in the continual struggles they faced when attempting to integrate into a society which they felt shunned them.

But, despite the improvements in the women's circumstances, Maria remains deeply concerned about her children.

'My two eldest children are without jobs and I worry about them and what they will do with their future. I have spent most of the time bringing up the children alone. I did not realize it before, but when we left Sudan we brought our problem with us.

'In a normal situation the African man would be head of the family, but my husband, Walter, has chosen to fight for his people, rather than just his own children.

'They are our children, we brought them into the world and so we have a responsibility to look after them. At least, one day they should be able to say, "My mother tried to do this," or "My father tried to do that."

'They still don't really feel part of this society but, even so, I don't think they would want to go back to Sudan.'

Yet Maria still has hopes of returning to the country she calls home.

'I will always be yearning to go home and I am always praying for peace. I have to believe that we will once again have peace in my country. Then I will go home. Even if I have to live under a tree it will be better for me. My body is here but my mind and spirit are back in Sudan. In a funny kind of way, I am living in two different worlds.

'Right now I have no country, I don't have a passport. I belong to the United Nations; they hold my passport and I have a travelling document. I am a displaced person.'

Maria's life has been riddled with pain and conflict, but she refuses to remain a victim. Her Christian faith provides her with an inner peace on which she draws in times of trouble, and she maintains a balance which enables her to keep her emotions under control.

'I don't have much time to think about the things I would enjoy doing, like dancing to the rhythm of the African drums. But I like helping people and that is something I feel that I must do.

'But what has really helped me is that in some way I am a negative person. I don't often get excited unless something hits me in the heart. I prefer to take my time to think over things. We will not always be here and it is better for us to take time to do what needs to be done.

'With two jobs and my voluntary work, I hardly have time to stop and think. If I was at home I would sit quietly by the river and watch it flow over the rocks. The river is my friend.'

In spite of the difficulties – and there have been many – Maria has found help and support from women she has met from different backgrounds, but she often feel frustrated by their lack of awareness of the lives of women in the South.

'The world is changing very fast and I feel that as women we must take it upon ourselves to learn about other countries and not just to judge people out of ignorance.

'We are from Africa, we are refugees, but we are also human beings. I blame the media for the images that are portrayed. All I see is starving children, poor children, poor houses, death and wars. Where is the gold, where is the oil, where is the fish that my people are dying for? Why isn't anyone promoting that? In every country we see only disaster; the positive side we don't see.

'I miss my family, and I hope that one day I will see them again.'

Until then, Maria Kwawang will continue to strive to secure a future for her children and to help others who have fled from a life of terror to a life of uncertainty and hardship.

'Only last week, three women and their children came to my house. They cannot speak English and were feeling isolated and afraid. They don't understand most of what is happening around them.

'Being in exile is not something I would wish on anyone. I will do what I can to help these women and their children. But I will not tell them, for now, that every day I still have to swallow a bitter pill and can only hope that it will not poison me.'

The bus slows; it is Maria's stop. The residential nursing-home is only a short distance away and Maria walks briskly and purposefully to start yet another eight-hour shift.

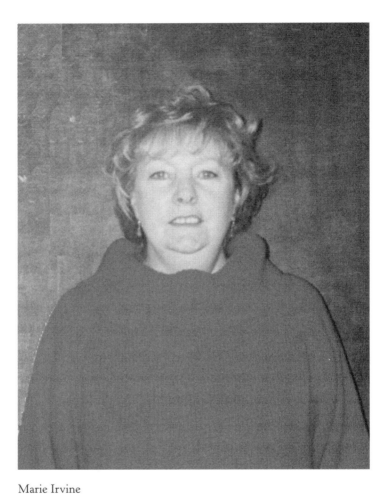

Marie Irvine

4   With Power and with Love

It is a damp and grey morning in July 2000 and the light breeze, cooler than expected for the time of year, is lifting old newspapers and crisp bags from the deserted pavements. It is the marching season, and the streets of Belfast are now free from the barricades that were symptoms of escalating violence the night before. But there remains an uneasy calm. Although no one knows quite what will happen next, a climate of fear has replaced the hope and reconciliation that were so fervently promoted by supporters of peace in the months that followed the agreement between the majority of political parties in Northern Ireland.

Half a dozen women are seated in Marie Irvine's living-room on the council estate called the Victoria Parade; it is off the New Lodge Road in north Belfast. Their discussion of the current situation is interrupted by the penetrating screams of a child in the back streets between the terraced houses. After a short pause, they continue to talk: the years of hearing the anguished cries from victims of violence have enabled them to know, in an instant, the difference between the sounds of prankish 'blackguarding', plaintive wails, and a child in danger.

Cups of tea are carried in by Marie's young daughter, Amy, and the women help themselves from the tray she puts carefully in front of them on the table in the middle of the room. Cigarettes are shared and a joke from Louisa, a prominent member of the group, lightens the rather pensive atmosphere.

Marie picks up her own cup of tea before leaning back into the well-padded sofa. She smiles at her colleagues, who are all from the Women's Centre, and reflects on when her own family used to sit around to have tea and conversation in the same way, almost thirty-four years ago.

A fair-skinned woman with lightly streaked brown hair and blue eyes, Marie is the eldest of four children. Her mother, Kate, also known as Kitty, toiled barefoot in the spinning-mill from the age of fourteen and worked her way up to become a supervisor. That was quite an achievement because it was at a time when women had little status. Her father, Johnny, worked as a postman when he left the army. Due to policies that led to the scarcity of housing for Catholics, like many others they shared a four-bedroom rented house with members of their extended family.

'My mummy and daddy were two wonderful people, and even though we didn't have a lot they made sure that we were never left wanting for anything.

'We lived with my granny Irvine in a three-bedroom house in Upton Street, part of an area known as Carrick Hill that is situated at the bottom of the Shankill Road and is a Catholic district. She was a great cook and used to bake potato and soda bread and cakes for the whole community.

'At that time, my mummy and daddy were very active in our community and would often tell us when we were small that we were never to judge people by their race, colour or creed and that we should always give a helping hand to those who needed it.'

At the onset of the troubles in the 1960s, Kate and Johnny Irvine remained examples of tolerance in a community that was being torn apart by sectarian violence. They were a respected couple, and their friends came from different parts of the community. However, Marie, her two sisters, Briege and Pat, and her brother, Sam, did not know the full extent of their parents' benevolence until they were adults.

'My parents used to visit elderly people who needed help in the area or were afraid to go out of their houses because of the troubles. Sometimes my mummy would go and pick up their messages [groceries]. If some people had money problems, my mummy would at least make sure they had food. She was young in her outlook and people of all ages would come to her for advice. Mummy was a carer and a sharer.

'No matter how bad things were, she would always say that one day the troubles would end, that we would live in a happier place and that we would have all the rights that we wanted. We believed her.'

Marie was greatly influenced by her parents' kindness and decided that she, too, wanted to contribute to the welfare of the community, without prejudice and across the religious divide. At sixteen, she started her voluntary work, and was part of a group that worked through numerous nights providing first aid to people who had been shot, and even removing bullets.

As the civil unrest increased in 1970, she set about organizing activities for young people who were out on the streets and vulnerable in a hostile and vengeful environment. In her eagerness to create a safe haven for them, she did not consider the dramatic change in the attitude of the Catholic community to the British soldiers – who had initially been seen as protectors from the Protestant mobs who had attacked and burnt many Catholic homes – or the dangers to herself.

'We started in an old gymnasium in a building which was used as an army barracks during the Second World War. It was a listed building and was used by the soldiers before it became a community centre; we called it The Recy which was short for Recreation Centre.

'We realized that it was best for the kids to be off the

streets and away from the dangers of the petrol bombs and shootings. The army helped us by providing a trampoline, and ran sessions with the kids on how to use it. They also taught them how to climb the bars against the walls and the ropes hanging from the ceiling. We had a lot of kids in the first few weeks, and then the numbers began to tail off.

'We found out that some of the older lads who were involved in organizations against the army had been warning off the kids. They had also been telling us young women not to associate with the soldiers, but I didn't think that they would go so far with the intimidation. The soldiers only wanted to help, but in the end we had to ask them to leave.

'The kids started to drift back to the club and everything went well for a while. Even the lads who had caused the soldiers to leave started to attend.'

Marie and her colleagues thought it was a good thing that the older lads, aged around eighteen, were also using the club, because it provided an alternative to becoming involved in the troubles brewing on the streets. But things turned sour when they became disruptive at a Hallowe'en party organized for the younger kids.

'We had worked hard on the costumes, and the delight and excitement on the children's faces made me determined that the mockery and jibes from these lads were not going to spoil things for them. I asked them to leave, and when they became abusive I literally shoved them out.

'At the end of the evening, when everyone had left, I locked up the building and began my way home, not knowing that these lads had been waiting outside for me. I only just turned the corner when they approached from behind and I was knocked to the ground. They beat me up and tugged at my hair, pulling out clumps of it that was never to grow back. I was left badly bruised and shaken, but still managed to make my way home.'

This was Marie's first real experience of the culture of

hatred that had lain hidden for years but was beginning to emerge during the troubles in Northern Ireland.

When she arrived home, she fell into her mother's arms.

'Mummy didn't tell my daddy what had happened to me because he was ill at that time and she knew that it would worry him. She told someone else instead, who was involved in the organization. Two of the boys got a hiding themselves and two others had to leave the country because of what they had done. I didn't want that to happen but that was how it was in those days.

'My mummy didn't want me to go back to the club after that, but I said there were kids out there who never had the love that I had, and anyway I wanted to continue what I had started. I remembered the look she gave me. It was as though she was looking back at herself. She then smiled and said softly, "Then be careful." '

Marie's childhood was a happy one, but she always felt the strain of being the eldest child. It was for her to set an example, even to her cousins, who were younger than she was. It was a responsibility she did not forget, and one that would stand her in good stead in the future.

The family was a close-knit one and Kate Irvine's determination to provide the best for her children led her to have their clothes made by a dressmaker on the Falls Road. While recognizing the sacrifices her mother had to make in order to pay for the tailor-made dresses for Marie and her sisters, it was something Marie hated because it made them stand out from other children. But she never complained, and the dresses later became a lesson in the importance of the preservation of another person's self-respect and dignity that her parents often talked about.

'Some of our clothes were given away to other children and my mummy used to say if we ever saw a child wearing our clothes we were never to say, "That was mine," and we never did.'

Kate Irvine had high hopes for all her children and wanted them to make a better life for themselves than she had working in the mills. Marie was a bright student and both her head teacher and her mother urged her to stay on at school for qualifications that would win her a place at university and possibly lead to a teaching career. But Marie chose work instead of study and, although she was very disappointed, Kate accepted her daughter's decision.

'It was in the sixties and everyone was leaving school to get jobs. Although there were plenty of jobs around, there were times when I went for an interview and didn't get the job because I was the wrong religion. It was hard for me to see other people with fewer qualifications getting the jobs that I had applied for.

'Once when this happened my daddy was so angry that he went to the place that had turned me down. The concierge, who was wearing a jacket with a row of medals, blocked his way and told him to leave. My daddy had been a colour sergeant in the Irish Fusiliers and told this rather stocky man that he had more medals than he had, but didn't need to wear them. He then said that he knew that I didn't get the job because I was the wrong religion and that he wanted to see someone in personnel.

'He didn't get to see anyone but he felt better that he had at least tried not to let their discrimination go unchallenged. I was glad of his support, but knew that little was going to change.'

In the early seventies, the troubles hastened the departure of many Catholics from Northern Ireland in search of work. Briege, Marie's younger sister, had already left for England and was settled in a job in London, working for a local authority.

Marie had just turned twenty-two when she joined her sister. She did not want to leave home but her mother thought it was important for her to have her independence and that her prospects in England were better.

'This was a big step for me and the three weeks that I was away I did nothing but cry for my mummy. I loved my daddy, but somehow all I could do was think of my mummy and remember her standing at the kitchen sink. She didn't look up when I was leaving but I remembered that my brother, Sam, had his arms around her. He had only just turned seventeen and he was saying, "It's all right, Mummy. After all, you still have me." I think that is what made me cry so much because I had never been away from home before.'

It wasn't long before Marie found a job with General Electric just outside Wembley in north-west London. She went out with Briege and some of her friends to celebrate on the Friday evening after her interview, and was looking forward to a new phase in her life. But her world and the plans for the future were to be shattered the following evening.

'It was early Saturday evening and there was a loud knock on the door. My Uncle Christie, who I was living with, answered it and two policemen were outside. They had come to tell us that there had been an explosion at McGurks, our local pub back home in North Queen Street, and that fifteen people were killed. My whole body seemed to cave in and my legs were too weak to hold me and so I sat down. I felt sick in my stomach as I thought about my daddy. I knew he always went to McGurks for a couple pints of Guinness every Saturday. My mummy didn't drink, but she would often go with my daddy and take an orange juice, so I didn't associate her with the blast and kept asking about my daddy. The police hadn't found him, but they had found my mummy. I asked them if she was in hospital and if she was all right. They said something but, although I could see their lips moving, I couldn't make out quite what they were saying. It was my uncle I heard telling me that they had found my mummy and that she was dead. He then left to collect Briege.

'I remember screaming and then I went into a dream and saw my mummy sitting on her own and going away on a ship. That was the last vision I had of her that night.'

Overwhelmed by guilt, thinking that if she had been at home her mother would not have died, Marie returned home to Belfast with Briege.

Marie had left her mother in the arms of her brother. Now, within a few short weeks, she was back but she could not even see her mother, who was in a closed coffin because she had been so badly burnt. It seemed too dreadful to be true.

Johnny Irvine had survived the explosion and had lain under the debris and rubble until a group of people dug him out. Thinking that he was to blame for Kate's death, because it was he who had been having the drink, he lay in his bed badly bruised, desolate, and unable to face his children.

Responding to his fear and the guilt he felt as a 'survivor', Marie comforted him and urged him to talk about the blast, thinking that it would help him cope with the tragedy. But her father's mind was a blur and he could only mumble, through the tears that rolled down his blistered and swollen face, about how he kept calling out for Kate, talking with her and thinking that she could hear him. Turning to her Granny Irvine, Marie was able to learn just how her mother had spent the last few hours of her life.

'Granny Irvine said that there was a distance about my mummy on the day she died, as if she had an inkling that something was going to happen. During the day my mummy went shopping with my daddy and bought two records. One was a favourite of mine, which I used to sing all the time at home, the other was a favourite of Briege's. Mummy didn't know this but just liked it because the record was playing in the shop at the time she went in.

'She put on my record first and put her head in her

hands and cried, "My Marie, my Marie." She then went upstairs, had a bath and said her prayers.

'When she was leaving she said to my granny, "Cheerio, Minnie, and take good care of yourself now." She had never said that before. On that particular evening she was late leaving the house and so called into the Recreation Centre on her way to meet my daddy. Normally, she would leave my daddy in the pub in time to get back to the Centre to say the rosary, as she was part of a group of women who were praying for peace. That evening she decided to go the Centre first.

'At the height of the troubles, my mummy used to say that we should never walk past someone who was lying injured on the streets. That we should use every humane bone in our body to help them if they were dying – and people were dying all around us. People would go out to work in the morning, and you didn't know if they would be coming home ever again. My mummy went out on the evening of 4 December 1971 and never returned.'

It was traditional for the head of the family to visit and pay their respects to other bereaved families, but Johnny Irvine was too ill and distressed to do so. Marie, assisted by an old boyfriend who had come to her aid on her return from London, had to take on that responsibility. Vivid memories of black flags on poles and outside windows remain in her mind. They served as a reminder of just how many families were suffering the way the Irvines were, and that the community had experienced a devastating loss of fifteen lives.

As her mother's funeral cortege passed through the streets of Belfast, thousands of people from all walks of life lined the streets. As it passed a factory which employed mostly Protestant workers, many of them hung out of the windows singing a famous song of the day, 'Bits and Pieces'. But this obscenity failed to mar the respect shown by many Catholics and Protestants for a woman who had devoted her life to her family and her community and for the others being buried that day. The coffin went past McGurks, where, amid the rubble, the only thing left hanging on a part of the wall that had survived the blast was a holy picture of the Sacred Heart.

Marie never returned to England. Instead, she took up the duty of caring for her family. Two years later she started her first job as a telephonist with the local exchange.

She then worked for a boutique, where the pay was small but enough to put food on the table and pay the bills. Briege returned to England and Marie did her best to hold the family together in the period of grieving that followed her mother's death.

'When my mummy was gone we lived under a cloud of gloom for a few years. My sister Pat was only fourteen when Mummy died and was going through a range of complex emotions we didn't know about, and my brother, Sam, who was seventeen, was also finding it a strain to keep going. My daddy and Granny Irvine, a spright wee woman of eighty-eight years, did what they could but there was a great void in our lives.

'A year later we lost Granny Irvine, and then my uncle, my father's only brother, died a year later. It was hard for my daddy because he had lost his wife, mother and brother in three years.'

It was during this most difficult of times that both Sam and Pat decided to get married. Pat was seventeen and pregnant with her first child.

Johnny Irvine tried to advise his daughter against an early marriage, saying that the child would be looked after, but Pat was headstrong and wanted her own family. For the first time since her mother's death Marie felt helpless. Pat had been traumatized by her mother's untimely and hor-rific death and, although Marie tried to talk with her, she dropped out of school and became more distant. Marie felt strongly that her sister was in search of love that would be a substitute for the love her mother had provided, and agonized over her decision to marry. There was little she could do but prepare herself to give Pat all the love and support she felt sure she would need in the future.

With Pat and Sam both married and settled in their own homes, Marie lived alone with her father, although her Aunt Mary, whose marriage had broken down, was to join them later.

Now that she no longer had to shoulder the full responsibilities for her younger brother and sister, life became a little easier for Marie, and after a number of administrative jobs, and one as a shop assistant, she settled as a bookkeeper for a man who owned a number of businesses in and around Belfast. But the terror of the bombs was never far away.

'By this time the troubles had intensified and both Loyalists and Republicans were bombing army installations and many places in the centre of the city. At one time you could be getting on with your work and suddenly, if you were lucky, an alarm would go off and you would have to run for safety.

'North Street Arcade ran right behind where my office was and one day a bomb went off without warning. I was lucky because I had only just got up from my desk and was shocked to see the large jagged pieces of glass from the shattered window that had landed on my desk. But that wasn't all I saw. The blast had brought with it a male torso that shot across the room and landed on the ledge of another window. There were no arms or legs and I couldn't remember if there was even a head. A young man who had been walking through the arcade at the time had been blown up. I was frozen to the spot and couldn't move my eyes from the horror in front of me.

'It took a few years, after my mummy's death, before I realized that I had been doing things without really thinking about them. I was looking after my daddy, the house, making sure that food was on the table and going out to work. The fact that bombs were all around us and were an everyday occurrence had not sunk in. But when I saw the torso the reality of my life suddenly hit me and I was in deep shock. My boss had to literally pick me up and take me into another room.

'The ambulance arrived and they wanted to admit me for observation, but I didn't want to go and within a few hours I was OK and went out drinking with my friends.'

Marie thought she had escaped the psychological damage such a terrible incident might well have inflicted and, deciding that she had to enjoy whatever time she had, in view of the uncertainties and dangers that surrounded her, she began to build herself a social life.

'There is a period of my life that is totally blank, but I do remember going to work and then straight on to the pub for a few drinks. If I did go home after work it was only to check on my daddy.'

Without her realizing it, the 'few drinks' soon became several, and Marie's dependency on alcohol as a means of coping with her daily existence was growing. It was during this time that she began to develop a relationship with a man who was to become the father of her child.

'When I first met him, Amy's dad was a charmer, a bit of a ladies' man who liked his drink. He was the manager at the poolroom at the bottom of the building where I worked in North Street. He was going through a divorce at the time and needed a shoulder to lean on. We became very good friends, and later on we developed a more intimate relationship. I really thought I had found someone special in him.'

But it was not long before the spectre of violence loomed large over the relationship. From early on, Marie was aware of the man's temper but she blamed the drink for his outbursts. As in other areas of her life, Marie chose denial as a way of coping, but it was only a matter of time before she was confronted by the true nature of her partner's violent tendencies.

They had been out drinking with friends and on the way home an argument developed. He pinned Marie against a wall and attacked her, before pulling her along the street. The episode left Marie feeling tense and very frightened. There were similar incidents during the time they were together, but none so serious that Marie thought she should end the relationship.

Domestic violence was an issue that was greatly ignored during the troubles in Northern Ireland and it was not until the early nineties that it emerged as a topic for reports by the academics and statisticians, who had previously been preoccupied by violence of a political kind. But it was to become a personal and troubling issue for Marie. She had grown up in a loving home, where her parents had their differences but had shown great respect for each other. The concept of a violent relationship was alien to her and when Amy's father first struck her – where the bruises could not be seen – she continued to blame his actions on drink and his feelings of inadequacy.

They had been together for three years when she agreed to go with him to the Isle of Man to find work.

'Amy's dad was an intelligent man but his drinking meant that he wasn't able to hold down a job. When we went to the Isle of Man for a summer season, I was given a post at the hotel as an assistant chef and he had a job as a dishwasher. Effectively I was his boss, and he found this difficult to handle.

'I tried to be sympathetic because I thought I loved him, but my emotions, although I didn't know it at the time, were ones of pity.'

The violence intensified and Marie found herself in a situation which was both unyielding and increasingly dangerous. The confusion around her predicament was compounded by the growing realization that she was rapidly becoming only a shadow of her former self.

'I felt ashamed and tried to cover the bruises. I then found out that I was pregnant. I was afraid to tell him, because for some reason I thought he would be angry.

'Then one night he came in after he had been drinking and I didn't think that I was going to survive the severe beating that he gave me. For a short time, as I lay on the floor, I thought about what happened to me when I was at the youth club, but that was nothing compared to what I was experiencing then.

'I remembered cowering and putting one hand up to cover my face and the other to cover my stomach. But he kept kicking me and I felt these heavy boots raining down onto my stomach and then onto my face. He just kept kicking and punching and I was afraid that I would lose the baby. I couldn't think why this was happening to me and I just kept praying for him to stop. When eventually he did, I managed to haul myself up to the bathroom and was sick. I lost my baby.'

Marie was taken to hospital. Her skull was X-rayed and it was found that her nose was fractured. She was unable to go out for six weeks as she allowed the bruises and the cuts on her face to heal. The scars on her face, which required many stitches, are visible to this day. But more grievous are the emotional ones that only Marie, in time, may be able to remedy.

Her boss was sympathetic and threatened to put Amy's father off the island, but in spite of all that had happened Marie made excuses for him and asked for him to be allowed to stay. She did, however, accept the offer to move to another room in the hotel. When the season was over she was relieved to be going home and she decided not to tell her father or any other member of her family about the brutality that she had experienced. The cruel reality about her relationship was to remain hidden and Marie stayed in the relationship until Amy was born.

'I remember when Amy was born in May 1984 and when she was put into my arms. I cried as I held her. She was so beautiful, and so fragile that I suddenly realized that I had to protect her. Her father had been out drinking and when he came to visit me he said that we should get married. I said no, because I didn't want this beautiful wee baby to be brought up in an abusive relationship.

'It was only then that I realized that I was being abused. Many women have a story to tell about abuse. I would have said years ago that I would never let a man hit me, but it is different when it happens to you. You feel powerless, you feel as though you can't hit back, and then you blame yourself, you say, "I made him do that, I made him go out to drink, I made him kick me."

'To protect my child I knew that I had to protect myself. I found the strength, there and then, to tell him to leave.'

By this time, unable to settle back in London since her mother's death, Briege had returned home. Amy was to be brought up in a loving home with Marie's father, Johnny, Briege and Marie's Aunt Mary giving a helping hand.

It was to be a new start for Marie, another step; but one she would take with the support and love of her family.

At the age of thirty-five, Marie decided that she would return to education, and she encouraged a few other women she knew to join her. They went to the Recy, where several courses that led to academic qualifications were being run.

'We took English language and literature, and although we all enjoyed reading, one or two of the older women didn't care much for dissecting the texts, and found English literature a wee bit tedious.

'Our male tutor was really into *Macbeth* and when he quoted the part where Lady Macbeth said, "Unsex me here", some of the older women were confused. They simply could not make sense of the point he was trying to make about Lady Macbeth saying that her circumstances would have been different had she been a man. In fact, it was too much for one woman, who later decided not to continue with the course.

'It was hard going having to study and care for a wee baby, but I stuck to it and got two good passes in both the language and literature courses.'

Marie's achievements not only reactivated the altruistic impulse that had lain dormant since the deaths of her mother and Granny Irvine, but also provided the perfect stimulus for her to continue to seek further qualifications. A six months' course in Politics, Sociology and Economics at the University of Ulster was the one that steered her towards a new career in community development.

During the years that followed, Marie took a training director's course through the Open University and Training Employment Agency. She then worked with Action for Community Employment (an agency which promoted jobs for long-term unemployed people), taught basic literacy and numeracy skills, established a Family and Women's Centre and got a position as a training officer with a national single parents' charity. Her generous and sympathetic reputation soon spread, and people came to her for advice as they had come to her mother.

The International Fund for Ireland recognized her dedication and service to the community and funded her to make a series of visits to community projects abroad to share her experiences and to learn from theirs.

'It all really started when as women we began to share our experiences of the troubles. What might have seemed horrific to people outside Northern Ireland for us were everyday occurrences and we all had our own way of coping.

'As we talked about the violence around us, some of the women started to talk about the abuse they had also been experiencing in their homes. It was then that I decided to share my own experiences, and everyone seemed to be taken by surprise that I too had been involved in a violent relationship.

'Once I told my story, the women began to trust me. I had come through it, I was a survivor, but I couldn't have done it without the support of my family. Many of the women didn't have that support and were even ashamed, like I was, to talk about what had happened to them. Something had to be done and so I set up a support group.'

To women at the Recreation Centre, Marie appeared an unlikely victim of domestic violence because her vigour and strength of character were the qualities to which they aspired. It was through her revelation that they were able to see that she was just like them.

The two-tone chime of the doorbell is heard above the women's voices, and Amy leaves the group to answer it. Isabel Nolan comes in and is welcomed by everyone. She is in her mid-sixties, and has known Marie for thirty-five years.

'Marie was a little older than my own children. She was a beautiful young woman and my fondest memories are of her when she used to model tights. She was gorgeous, and I remember her lovely legs in the wee short skirts.

'Although we lived close by, I didn't see much of Marie after her mummy died, but I caught up with her again when she was pregnant with Amy. I was an only child and was very depressed when my own mother died. I was able to talk to Marie about my feelings and she helped me a lot.'

Isabel Nolan was one of the women Marie had encouraged to join her for classes at the Recreation Centre. Mrs Nolan was reluctant at first and had expected Marie to call for her, as it was a big step for a woman of her mature years to be taking. But Marie didn't call.

'Marie is one of those people who will encourage you up to a point and leave the rest to you. I was very nervous at first but Marie and all the other women were great. To me it was all a bit of fun and a chance to meet other women, so when I passed the exams with good grades I was surprised.'

Like many other women, Mrs Nolan found a good friend in Marie and joined in some of her community work. She also became a member of the women's group that Marie established.

'Marie always works hard behind the scenes for women – any woman who wants to get back into education, Marie will fix that up. Many women might be a little nervous, thinking that education is not for them, but I was fifty when I did my English exam. My mother would probably have turned in her grave to think I was doing exams at that age, but this is what it is all about. Marie helped me to realize that it's never too late to try something new.

'She is very strong and won't let obstacles get in her way. Marie is the driving force behind us.'

Encouraged by Marie, Mrs Nolan took a qualification in adult literacy and became a tutor. Meeting some of her former students, who are now progressing in their own careers, makes her proud.

'I remember meeting one of my first students a few years ago. She had dropped out of school, like so many others did during the height of the troubles. In those times it was hard to make young people see the value of an education when there were no jobs for them.

'This wee student was married with three children and was having difficulties at home. Her husband was an alcoholic and would say that he was paying the bills when in fact he was spending the money on drink. She couldn't read, and so had to rely on him. Then one day he just walked out, leaving her to cope with all the children and the bills he said he had been paying.

'She wanted to help her children with their homework but couldn't, and so she started to come to classes. Now she is doing very well for herself and her children.

'I had time on my hands and Marie got me started. I achieved and was then able to help other women to do the same. In many ways, Marie has helped to change the lives of women she doesn't even know about.

'She is always thinking about other people. Right now she is developing plans for improving the area, bringing in more greenery so that people can feel proud about where they live. We will all benefit from that.'

Flowers arrive for Marie: the women want to show how much they appreciated her year's work as they begin their two-week summer break. It is a total surprise and Marie thanks them as she admires the pink and white carnations, freesias and chrysanthemums.

The Women's Drop-in Centre is only a year old but already many women have benefited. Working across communities and with other women's groups, members talk about 'bread-and-butter issues' like solvent and drug abuse and what should be done about them. They share what they learn from other quarters, like the fact that many expectant young mothers are starving themselves so that they can have small babies they can treat like dolls. Such information helps to guide the women working with teenage mothers. Domestic violence and child abuse, which are prevalent in their communities, are vigorously discussed. They look at provision for lone parents and raise money for crèche and childcare facilities. They have started sewing and knitting classes and encourage women to venture into small and community businesses.

Some women enjoy attending the group for the *craic* (conversation), because it takes them out of their isolation and enables them to share, often for the first time, the painful loss of a loved one.

'So many women have someone who has died in the troubles, a mother, brother, father or sister. One woman's brother was shot as he was organizing the fruit shelf in his shop. When she was twelve, another woman saw her friend, after he said he didn't care if he lived or died, shoot himself in the head. This incident stayed with her for twenty-five years.

'There's no counselling, so women carry their grief for years. Now, through listening, we are helping each other to heal.'

Marie has become a mentor, and someone to admire, but the personal cost has been high.

'I have a weakness in my heart – it's hereditary – and when I took my first heart attack at the age of thirty-seven, my daddy said that was enough and I should stop working. I knew I was taking on too much but there was a lot to do. Many people needed help and support and I knew that I could provide it.

'I promised my daddy I would slow down. He said he would make sure I did and promptly took the telephone plug out from the wall.'

But it wasn't long before Marie was back into her routine of providing help wherever it was needed in and around her community, and also making sure that she gave time to Amy, who had just started school.

Within a couple of years, Marie suffered another and more serious heart attack and, knowing that she would be lucky to survive a third, at last decided to cut her workload. But there were even more testing times ahead.

'My daddy died of a heart attack in 1994. I went home after work to leave the car before going on to a friend's party and when I was leaving he simply said, "Be careful and mind yourself." When I got back I was told that he had died in the house with Amy and Briege.

'I didn't see him until the next day, when he was brought back to the house in a coffin. I was broken-hearted. He was a great man and, like my mummy, he had the respect of people from all backgrounds.

'As a colour sergeant he had trained many officers who were themselves part of the British Army. One day a major who was with some of the soldiers came over to my daddy and asked if he remembered him. My daddy said yes and took him for a drink.

'When he was leaving, he shook hands with this young man and told him that if he was to see him again he wasn't to speak to him because it would be dangerous for both of them. I know that was very painful for him.

'He never complained and always did the best he could for his family. He even gave up his pension so that he could buy a pram for me when I was a baby.

'My daddy never really got over my mummy's death and there were times when he was asleep that he would raise both his arms slightly, moving them as though he was trying to push something away from him. After a while we realized that he was reliving the explosion at McGurks.'

With little time to grieve for her father, Marie was soon having to arrange the funeral of her Aunty Mary, who died six months later.

'I still don't know how we kept going. The sudden deaths of two people we loved so much had been traumatic, but somehow we got through it. I think we just had to survive for each other. I also knew that I had to be strong for my wee daughter, who was depending on me.'

For the next few years Marie was able to keep a better balance between her paid and voluntary work. Things became easier when she managed to raise the funds required to devote herself fully to work with women.

Then, in August 1998, came the Omagh bombing, which killed twenty-nine people.

'I remember being glued to the television at the time of the Omagh bombing. My body was shaking and I had a deep feeling of sorrow for the families of those people who died.'

When she went to bed that night, the memories of traumatic experiences in her own life came back to Marie. As she tried to sleep, she relived the terror and the guilt of the events that she had only dealt with outwardly in order to continue with her daily life.

'Then the next morning I took a nervous breakdown. I simply couldn't get out of bed, I couldn't wash myself, I couldn't speak, I couldn't even walk.

'The media coverage of the Omagh bombing had triggered something off in my brain that I had hidden for almost thirty years. I hadn't done my grieving for my mummy, and the psychiatrist said I had actually seen my mother's death in a flashback and these things in my brain had disintegrated, as I couldn't cope with it.

'It was a terrible time for Amy to see me in that way, it was a terrible time for my sisters to go through, but I had their help.

'I was a woman who had been out working, I was a trainer in helping people through the grieving process, and yet I never stopped to think or try to understand what was happening to me.'

Once again, and with the support of her family, Marie recovered. The breakdown had forced her to come to terms with the tangled emotions within herself that her work with others had concealed.

She had at last to face the many things she had shrugged off as just another episode; like the time when she would have been killed had she stepped out of her office to visit an elderly woman in a Protestant area. (A colleague at work had been informed that members of a notorious gang would be waiting outside the office to abduct another Catholic at the height of the Shankill Butchers gang's reign of terror. Marie's high-profile community work had made her a target.) She had still to face the guilt

over her mother's death, which haunted her. The fact
that her father had died while she was celebrating with
friends. The fact that she had kept from her daughter,
Amy, the violence she experienced from her father and
the loss of a baby who might have been a brother or sister to
her. That her little sister, Pat, had herself been in a violent
relationship and she had not done enough to help her.

'It took some time for me to work through all these
things and maybe there are more. I have learnt a lot
through my experiences but didn't take time to look at how
I had been affected by them.'

Amy, now sixteen, hugs her mother. 'I have always been
proud of my mummy. It must have been hard for her coping with all that she did when I was a wee baby. She often
has a lot to worry about but she never stops until she has
achieved what she sets out to achieve.

'Sometimes I do worry about her when she is taking on
too much, and I even get angry because I can see that she is
wearing herself down. But I also see that she needs to do
what she does.

'I hope that I will be strong enough to help other people
like she has.'

The women say their good-byes and Marie begins to
arrange the flowers in a vase she takes from a cupboard in
her small kitchen.

'As women, I think we go through conflict every day of
our lives, with children, husbands, partners, work and
many other things.

'Women are strong, and a lot of our strength comes
from what we have experienced. We do have a lot of power,
and we should learn to use that power with love. It's the
love, the power and enthusiasm for everything around us
that I believe is important.

'It is the enthusiasm that keeps me going, the eagerness
to help another person, because in doing that I am helping
myself.

'Sometimes I get lonely, and there are times when it would be great to have a man put his arms around me, comfort me and say, "Marie, I will help with this or that." But I don't dwell on that, especially when I realize that I get a lot of love from my family, the kind of love that has come through generations. Sometimes I don't feel like doing anything and say to myself that I can't be bothered, but we have a women's instinct that says, "Get on with it and enjoy it."

'No matter who we are, where we are in the world, or what we experience as women, it is that inner strength that pulls you through.'

Marina Beyer

5 *A Time to be Me*

Marina Beyer sits with a colleague in a bar-restaurant at Brunnenstrasse 27 in East Berlin. Marina, a slight woman with short blond hair, is discussing the morning's work with Katrin Wolf. It is the first day of a three-day conference to consider the roles of women who work within their neighbourhoods; almost fifty women have travelled from Russia, Poland, the Ukraine and Romania to attend.

The women talked about their personal lives, the political and economic situations as well as the poor social conditions in their countries. Despite the dramatic changes that have taken place in the political landscapes of Eastern Europe, for most people the circumstances are still grim, with high unemployment among men and limited opportunities for women. It is still too early to tell how much the women have taken from one another's experiences, but what is clear is their willingness to share and to listen.

Katrin has to leave to prepare for the afternoon's session, but Marina is in no hurry and orders a beer before she lights another cigarette. Drawing parallels with her own life, she reflects on what she has heard during the morning. Like many of the women involved in the training programme, Marina has a story to tell.

She was born in East Berlin, then the capital of the German Democratic Republic (GDR), in 1950 and was brought up by her mother, Elsbeth, and her grandmother,

Frieda Grasse. Her father, Josef Loew, an Austrian who worked in the GDR, never lived with her mother.

'My father was a charming and well-educated man. He was already married when I was born and had no intention of leaving his wife to be with my mother and me. But he would always visit me on my birthdays and bring presents. Sometimes he would send an official car to take me to his office and we would have some time together then. I never really knew what it was like to have a real father, someone who was always there for me.'

Brought up in a house of women, Marina only heard stories from her mother, grandmother and aunts, about the man who was to become her role model. He was her grandfather, Paul Grasse. He came from a very poor background. He was born in a working-class neighbourhood in Berlin in 1885; his mother was a *Waschfrau*, a washerwoman, and she was a single mother. He was a member of the Communist Party, and became a member of the Preussische Landtag (the regional parliament). After 1933, when the Nazis won the elections in Germany and the Communist and the Social Democratic Parties were banned, he went into exile, first in Prague and then in Paris. He was active in the French resistance until 1943 when he was arrested and sent to the notorious Buchenwald concentration camp.

'My grandfather was my hero because all the women in my family had put a lot of energy into protecting him from the Nazis. They lived in fear, knowing that the Nazis could come at any time and question them about him. Even though they were threatened with imprisonment, the women never disclosed his whereabouts. They were very courageous women and my grandmother, who always knew where my grandfather was, used to take messages to him across the border. She wasn't political but did it for love.

'The women in my family were poor, had babies but had no money and no jobs. Several times, they were all thrown out of a very small flat because they could not pay the rent.

Protecting my grandfather was possibly the only constant thing in their lives, and so it was important for them to tell stories about him.

'When my grandfather worked for the parliament as deputy, once a year they got money [Diäten]. He spent much of it on my grandmother, buying her expensive clothes and taking her to the opera.

'He was a very kind man, and once when my mother was in hospital with tuberculosis he bought her a gold ballpoint pen. Two weeks later he saw the same pen in a second-hand shop [Pfandleihe] after my grandmother had sold it and used the money to buy food. He had wanted the best for his family but this made him realize the price they had to pay for his political activities.

Paul Grasse lived for only six months after he returned from the concentration camp at the end of the war. Before his death in January 1946 he asked Marina's mother, Elsbeth, the youngest of his three daughters, to look after his beloved wife. Families composed solely of females were not uncommon in the postwar German Democratic Republic, as there were then 135 females to every 100 males. As men like Paul Grasse and prisoners of war returned, this disproportion diminished but even as late as the early 1980s females still outnumbered males by 112 to 100.

Paul Grasse's final request proved a lifetime burden for Elsbeth, who was then aged thirty-two.

When Marina's mother became pregnant with her, Frieda Grasse was angry with her daughter and boxed her ears, but after Marina was born she became a proud grandmother, and was more than happy to look after Marina while Elsbeth went out to work.

They lived in a flat in Prent Lauer Berg, a typical working-class district in East Berlin. There were four apartment blocks and Marina lived in the first block, which had belonged to a Nazi family until the end of the war. Her grandmother and mother had been given the flat in recognition of their involvement in the resistance. It had three big bedrooms and was well furnished with heavy, dark furniture.

Like her father, Elsbeth became a political activist and was often busy with Party matters, which provided relief from a quarrelsome Frieda.

'My mother was very organized and had a strong sense of duty and responsibilities, which is what I think helped her to cope with my grandmother, who was very demanding. They had a very complicated relationship and often argued. Sometimes it was difficult for me to witness the distress of the two people I loved so much.'

Elsbeth's busy life left her with little time to spend with the young Marina, and it meant that the times they had together were precious to both of them.

'I remember seeing my mother only when she came home from the office in the evenings, and then we had little time because I had to go to bed. But Sunday afternoons were different.

'My mother used to manicure her nails each Sunday and I would sit on a stool by her feet as she told me stories about the old days. She had a great sense of humour and we had a lot of fun together. I loved her voice; it was soft and gentle compared to my grandmother's, which was loud and coarse.

'I loved listening to the stories. Many of them were about my grandfather. But sometimes they gave me nightmares. I used to dream about him. I would see him as a tormented prisoner; I dreamt of the raids on our home to find him, when my grandmother used to be beaten by the Gestapo; and of the swastika. Some nights I would wake up soaked with sweat, but I never told my mother or my grandmother about these nightmares.'

The young Marina did not like nursery school, mainly because she had to eat everything on her plate and there was no grandmother to look after her. For a time, her cousin Bernd, who was at the same nursery, looked after her. Then, without warning, he left with his family overnight, the first of a number of Marina's relatives to move to West Germany, which was just a few yards away from where she lived.

The bridge that led to the West was called the 'Bad Bridge' and to Marina this meant that what lay beyond it must be bad, even slot machines for chewing-gum, which were objects of desire for the young Marina. Years later she learnt that the Bad Bridge was named after the architect Bose, which translated as 'bad'.

For a child of five years old, this was a very confusing time.

'I couldn't understand what was going on. When I was a child I believed that the West was where the Nazis were and that we in the East were all in the Communist Party and had been fighting against them. It was unthinkable for me that people from my own family were going to the West.

'A man living in the flat below us had been sent to a concentration camp like my grandfather, and he had a number on his arm. My grandmother was disparaging about him and said that he was a Jew, and yet he was also a communist.

'One day, when I was playing outside in the backyard, a woman shouted at me, "Go away – you are a communist." I couldn't understand that somebody would be shouting at me to go away.

'I asked her why she was shouting at me like this when I was a communist and living in the East. She didn't give me an answer.'

From nursery school, Marina went to a school on Ibsenstrasse, which was nearer the Bad Bridge. It was not unusual to find that pupils were absent in the morning because their parents had decided to leave for the West.

Many teachers also went absent; those who remained said they were socialists and suggested that the children should become the same.

It was customary for every child to be involved in the Young Pioneers, a GDR youth organization which was supposed to introduce the next generation to socialist ideology.

When, at six years old, Marina became chair of the Young Pioneers, she felt that Paul Grasse would have been proud of her.

'In the Young Pioneers we not only held meetings but also took part in many different events. I remember the first of May, which was a working-class day in Berlin, and I went with my mother to a big demonstration. I was happy and proud to be wearing my uniform because I was a fighter for socialism. But, more than that, I felt sure that my mother would buy me a sausage and an ice cream.'

Some of Marina's fellow pupils hated her because of her position in the Pioneers. They made fun of her and called her a 'bespectacled communist brat'. For Marina it was a painful experience, which remains with her to this day.

'Only three of us in the class had parents who were members of the Communist Party, and some of my *Mitschüler* [schoolmates] hated us for that, particularly two boys named Schulle and Radtke, who tormented us. Every morning before register they would call us out to stand in front of the class and then they would ask if we wanted to have twenty thumps on our arms or on our legs. This went on for three or four months.

'I remember thinking about my grandfather, Paul Grasse, and knowing that I had to be strong like him. Every morning I had in my mind that I would not cry. I would say to myself, "You are like your grandfather, you are a hero and you will not cry." But one day it hurt so much that I did cry and I didn't want to go to school the next morning.'

Frieda was worried about her granddaughter, and seeing her distress she sat quietly with her and made her talk about all that had been taking place. After hearing Marina's story Frieda decided that she would go to the school the next morning and confront the two boys.

'I couldn't sleep the whole night because to me the very idea of my grandmother coming into the school to defend me was a catastrophe. But I could do nothing and she would not listen to me when I asked her not to go.'

Frieda marched into the schoolyard with Marina the next morning and demanded that she point out her tormentors.

'The boys were standing at the far end of the schoolyard and as my grandmother approached them they began to run. She was by then an old woman but she picked up her skirt and began to chase after them. I knew that she had no chance of catching them. They were laughing as they kept running further away from her.

'It was a terrible sight. I just didn't like to see my grandmother in this undignified way. I knew that she could only lose and I was worried that she would fall over. She didn't catch them, and things got worse for me and I got more thumps than the others.'

One morning when Marina arrived at school she learnt that both the boys had disappeared to the West. The flight of the boys and their families across the Iron Curtain only served to confirm in her mind that everyone who was bad would eventually end up going to the West across the Bad Bridge. At last, she was free from the bullies.

Even though she had friends at school, Marina was often lonely. But at home the situation was different because she knew that she had the full attention of her mother and grandmother. Safe in this knowledge, she never thought that her position might be threatened; until Karl appeared on the scene.

'Karl was my mother's boyfriend. He was a big man and

used to tell lots of jokes. He always made a point of being very kind to me and bought me sweets. I knew that he was trying to win me over but I wasn't going to let him. I didn't want to share the little time I had with my mother with him or anyone else, and so I would not respond to his attentions.'

Each holiday period, Marina and her mother spent two weeks at a Baltic Sea resort. It was something she longed for because it was the only time during the year that she and her mother were alone together.

'We always had a wonderful time. I loved ice cream but, because we were poor, my mother could only buy me an ice cream every third day and I looked forward to this day very much. Then, on one of my "third" days, Karl turned up.

'I was about five years old and was very angry with my mother and could not believe that she didn't realize that he would spoil our holiday together. He kept talking to me and smiling but I didn't say anything back and I certainly didn't smile. He then took us to a café and bought me a very big ice cream, the best I had ever seen. It was in a tall glass, with chocolate and cherries around and an umbrella placed in the middle.'

Marina sat in the café with a stern look on her face and her arms folded as Karl placed the ice cream in front of her. She stared at it for a long time, and then looked at him with a frown.

'I knew that he was trying to buy my affections with this ice cream and decided that I would not eat it. This was the only chance I had to fight against my mother's lover and I took it. I felt like crying as the umbrella started to sink into the glass as the ice cream melted.

'The next morning Karl disappeared and I never saw him again.'

When she was ten, Marina became ill with a rare disease of the joints and found it difficult to walk. As the disease worsened, her skin was constantly inflamed and she was admitted to hospital, where she remained for several months. Although her mother and grandmother were regular visitors, her father never once visited. But she found out later that he had been very concerned about her.

'My father had spoken with the doctors and was trying to find out what would be the best treatment for me. He had also been making plans for me to go to Moscow, where he was advised that I could get better medical attention. In the end, the hospital tried a new therapy and I was cured.

'I knew that my mother was trying to make me feel better about him not visiting me, but it didn't really work because I would have preferred that he had been at my bedside with his arms round me.'

Within a few weeks of leaving hospital, Marina was back at school and, even though she had lost weight and felt ugly, she settled well into her studies. Life was once again comfortable in its routine, but whatever belief Marina had that she was returning to the world she had known before her illness was abruptly shattered one summer day.

'The [Berlin] Wall went up in August 1961, and I remember people crying and wailing in the streets. I didn't understand what was going on. It was on a Sunday and we had to move out of our flat. It was chaos. My grandmother kept saying how terrible this situation was, that my mother had to go to a Party committee meeting and that we were in a political crisis.

'It was hard for my mother, because her sisters and her very close friends lived in West Berlin and she was afraid that she would not see them again.

'I understood that something had to be done because people, particularly those who were educated, were all leaving. I had no interest in the West – it was not my country – but other people were no longer able to choose where they wanted to be.'

But unknown to Marina, her father had made his choice to move West several months before, after refusing to give up his Austrian identity to become a GDR citizen.

'My father came to see my mother before he left for Vienna with his wife. He told her that he was leaving and wanted to take me with them but she said no.

'Later, when she told me, I was upset and could not believe that he could have left without saying goodbye to me. I felt betrayed and abandoned.'

At eleven, Marina had to face a new phase in her life, one in which her father was no longer certain to visit on her birthday and in which she thought that she would never again see her relatives who had moved to the West. The Berlin Wall did more than divide Marina's city: it was also symbolic of how much smaller her world had become.

Seven years later, Marina was reunited with members of her family who had left for the West. The meeting was in Prague but it was not totally happy because of a disagreement that erupted over the Prague Spring, the experiment in democratic socialism that was at the core of President Alexander Dubček's government in 1968.

The Prague Spring, which entailed purging the government and Communist Party of the 'old guard' with reforms that were being forced by public opinion, had sent shock-waves through the Communist bloc. The Czechoslovak government and the Communist Party were to be made more democratic, and a revised constitution would guarantee civil rights and rehabilitate all those whose rights had been infringed in the past. Dubček called this 'socialism with a human face'.

'My mother and I got to know an elderly couple we met in a café who were communist intellectuals. They invited us to their apartment and told us about the changes in the Czechoslovak regime known as the Prague Spring. Our relatives from the West were upset that we had allowed ourselves to become involved with this couple, who were promoting the reforms, and felt that we were putting our-selves at risk, as we were still living in the East. But the couple had convinced my mother and me that we needed a socialism that allowed self-determination and for people to be treated with respect and dignity.'

But the Prague Spring was seen by the Soviet premier, Leonid Brezhnev, as a threat to Soviet dominance in East-ern Europe. On 20 August 1968 Soviet and Warsaw Pact forces invaded Czechoslovakia, and Dubček's govern-ment was overthrown. Czechoslovakia's experiment with democracy was brought to an abrupt end.

That same year, at the age of eighteen, Marina went to Potsdam near to Berlin to study *Pädagogik* [theory of edu-cation] at the university. Before starting the course, all stu-dents were required to sign a resolution endorsing the intervention of the 'Fraternal Socialist Parties' in Prague. Marina was a lone voice among forty students when she refused to sign. She argued for reform, but she received no support from the other students.

'I then heard someone say, "Anyone who is not for us is against us." This was something my grandfather used to say, and I was torn between what I believed and supported and the words that were ringing in my ears. I was in an impossible situation and realized that there was nothing I could do but sign.'

Marina felt that she had betrayed the cherished prin-ciples that had been passed down to her in her mother's and grandmother's recounting of the life of her grand-father, Paul Grasse. The anguish remained with her for months. She felt that she had been placed in a terrible dilemma: she did not want to be isolated from her peers and yet a voice within her argued that she should stand up for what she thought was right. In the end a young woman's need to be accepted outweighed her principles and values. Although the subject was never brought up again, Marina always felt that she was not fully trusted by other students. The environment was an uneasy one for someone who wanted change.

It wasn't long before Marina's resolve was once again put to the test.

'One day I was summoned by university officials to meet two men who introduced themselves as members of the State Security Service [the notorious Stasi]. They knew of my family background and that I held very strong views, and asked me to join them. I told them I wanted nothing to do with them, because I knew that they wanted me to become an informer.

'They offered to get me a good job after I left university and when I declined their offer they said that they could put obstacles in my way.

'I had betrayed myself once before and was not going to do it a second time. I thought of my grandfather and what he would do, but I knew that I had to decide for myself. In the end, I told them that I would not be bought and that I wasn't afraid of obstacles.

'They left me alone after that, although I always expected that they would try again some other time.'

There were indeed obstacles at university, but they were not of the Secret Service's making. On finding that the dictatorial and hierarchical education system went against almost everything she stood for in the aftermath of the Prague Spring, Marina could not settle into her studying. When she discovered that she had an abnormality of the vocal chords which could worsen at any time and prevent her from being able to speak, she took this as a sign that she was not meant to be a teacher and left.

Moving back to Berlin, Marina found a small apartment. It had an outside toilet and was by no means a grand place but it was close to her grandmother and mother; the latter was disappointed that her daughter had not decided to return home.

'It didn't seem to matter too much to my mother when I

left for university in Potsdam because I was living in the student hostels and there was always a place at home for me. When I decided to find my own place, my mother had to come to terms with the fact that I was no longer a little girl and that I wanted to take responsibility for myself.

'She was really too afraid to stay alone with my grandmother. Relationships had soured between them but I could no longer be the bridge between the two of them. I had my own life to live.'

In 1970, when she was more settled in her new surroundings, Marina enrolled at the University of Berlin to study biology. She was happy to be among like-minded students with whom she could talk about the political situation until the early hours of the morning. These conversations helped her to mature politically and clarify her thoughts so she could shed the ideology of her childhood. She still supported socialist ideals but felt that she could not make compromises of which she would be ashamed. She did not join the Communist Party, because she believed it was no longer the party her grandfather had fought for.

She graduated with honours and secured a position in the laboratory of the Institute of the Academy of Sciences. Her first meeting with the professor who was to be her superior was not a good one.

'He was a big man, with a round face and a grey beard. He was sitting behind an oak desk which reminded me of the heavy furniture we'd had in the apartment we were given when the Nazis left. His chair was much higher than the one I was given, and I was made to feel very small as I looked up at him. He was a most imposing figure.

'His voice seemed to boom across the room when he said, "If you propose to have children, this is not the place for you." I was astonished and told him that I had no intention of having children.'

But within a few months, Marina was pregnant. She had

met Joachim Fröhlich in the summer of 1973, during the
World Music Festival on Alexanderplatz, a year before she
graduated. She had liked the way he laughed, loudly and
infectiously, and had watched as he expressed his political
views and then listened attentively to others. She had been
standing with a group of friends and he caught her eye
once or twice and smiled. It was a warm and sensuous
smile.

She met him a second time in a jazz bar and within
months he had moved in with her, driven the rats out of
the toilet and installed a shower. In September 1975 their
first son was born and Marina called him Paul Grasse; a
year later came her second son, Benjamin.

Joachim, who was a computer analyst, supported
Marina in her work. Together with a few other friends, in
the early 1980s she established the Pankow Peace Circle, a
group which opposed the GDR's becoming more militar-
ized in response to NATO's 'twin-track' policy. Their activities soon attracted the attention of the fearsome State
Security Police, who immediately categorized them as hostile and negative. It was not long before Marina's superiors,
including the professor, were informed of what was taking
place. She was left in no doubt that they considered her
political activities a distraction from her work.

'It was a very hard time for me. I always seemed to be
fighting against a system that was able to recreate itself.
With all my work and two small children, Joachim and I
had little time to spend together, and although we loved
each other there was a feeling that it was just not enough.

'Then my mother was diagnosed with cancer and I had
also to look after her.'

Elsbeth Grasse died in 1980. She had suffered griev-
ously from a cancer which ripped through her body and
left her weak and badly emaciated.

'It was painful to see how my mother had suffered. She
had lived her life fighting for what she believed in and

taking care of my grandmother and me. I found myself wishing that life had been kinder to her and taking some of the blame for not allowing her the happiness she deserved.

'It was years before I could read the many letters that my mother had kept in a small box. I cried when I realized that her life had not been as solitary as I had imagined but that she had in fact found love, and not only with my father and Karl. The letters were endearing and I was happy to know that my mother had also been a woman.'

After her mother's death, Marina's sadness was compounded when she and Joachim parted. He had met and had fallen in love with another woman, whom he subsequently married. Feeling abandoned once again, Marina was left to bring up her children alone, although Joachim continued to visit.

Frieda Grasse hoped that Marina would take over where Elsbeth had left off in caring for her, and Marina did not disappoint her. The old woman lived with Marina and her great-grandchildren for nearly four years. During the last few weeks of Frieda's life, Marina found a place for her in a nursing-home where she was able to get the full care that she needed. The home was near where Marina lived and she visited her grandmother every day. Frieda died at the age of ninety-nine.

Marina continued her work with the Pankow Peace Circle, where she met Wolfgang Beyer. He had been in prison because he had refused to do military service on account of his deeply held religious beliefs. After his release he decided to become a priest.

Marina was a non-believer but she admired Wolfgang's quiet strength and his humour. He in turn loved her children and was able to provide her with a tenderness she had yearned for since the death of her mother. Within a year of having met, Wolfgang and Marina were married. Her third child, Johanna, was born in 1985, three years before

Marina obtained her doctorate in biology (behavioural science).

Finding herself pregnant again when Johanna was less than a year old, and thinking that she would not be able to cope, Marina sought advice from a friend who herself had four young children. Reassured, Marina was able to look forward to the birth, and her fourth child brought her much joy and happiness.

While Wolfgang studied theology Marina took extra leave from work to look after the children, which greatly displeased some of her superiors. The relationship between her and the professor deteriorated, not only because she had had the temerity to bear four children but also because of her continuing political activities.

When Marina was taken away for questioning by the Stasi, the professor felt that her position at the Academy was untenable and suggested that she should resign. Marina responded that she would leave in her own time.

The Pankow Peace Circle was persistently under surveillance by the Stasi and was often the target of informers, as it became one of the most important opposition peace groups in the GDR.

Although suffering constant harassment, its members gave each other a support which strengthened their determination to continue. They held closed and open discussions and public events, never once fearing repercussions. To Marina and Wolfgang, the Circle had become a second family.

Wolfgang supported Marina and shared the responsibilities of looking after the children and their home. He secretly hoped that she would embrace his Christian faith and be baptized, but she had no interest in becoming a convert.

When Wolfgang completed his studies and the Church demanded that she be baptized before he could be given his own parish, Marina was outraged that the Church authorities should attempt to have her compromise her own moral code, and refused to be blackmailed.

Although Wolfgang got his parish anyway, this was the first sign of the extent of her resistance to the Christian faith; it was eventually to drive a wedge between them.

Between 1987 and 1989 there were a number of protests which caused the government some concern, and when Hungary opened its border with Austria East German citizens flocked across, leaving everything behind them.

Marina wept as she watched television pictures of this exodus. Some of her friends from the Peace Circle took the opportunity to leave but she wanted to stay. The sense of duty that had remained with her from her days as a Young Pioneer told her there was work to be done at home.

As well as being involved in the peace movement, Marina was chair of an education reform group set up by the Round Table to hold a critical review of education.

'After the borders were opened, many people who were responsible for state education fled. This provided an opportunity to look at a new system of education that was more open, and where a culture of subservience could be challenged.

'We held a meeting in the Congress Hall at the Alexanderplatz on 9 November 1989. The hall was packed and it was a moving event. For the first time in many years, there was an exchange of views between teachers, parents, pupils, the old and the young. The atmosphere was charged and we could sense a grand new beginning.

'But as a rumour rippled through the hall that the Wall was open, people no longer wanted to discuss new education policies. Everyone wanted to go to the West.'

As millions of people throughout the world watched on their televisions, the Berlin Wall came down, profoundly affecting the political course of the late twentieth century.

Marina's prominent roles in the Peace Circle and other

opposition groups brought her to the attention of the Social Democratic Parliamentary Group, and she was summoned to an urgent meeting.

'When I arrived at the Volkskammer (parliament building), where this meeting was being held, a few people from the peace movement who I knew were also present.

'I was asked if I would like to be the new government's equal opportunities commissioner. I had no idea what this meant and when it was explained to me I was still thinking about it when I was being hurried to meet a panel of members of parliament to introduce myself and my ideas for making such a position a success.'

Marina talked about herself and her experience in the Peace Circle, and gave her views on an enlightened and open socialism. As she ended her presentation, she had a warm feeling inside her which said that this was possibly the moment for which all her previous experiences had been preparing her. She became aware that she could have a role in government and that her views could help shape a new and more democratic society.

She was still thinking about how such an office might develop when a question from a member of parliament (*Abgeordnete*) gave her the clarity she needed about her new role.

'There were around fifty MPs in the grand chamber. One of the men asked me how a mother of four children could assume such a position of responsibility in the government, and then went on to say that he suspected that it would be extremely difficult.

'I felt sure that the men who were present had not been asked about their children or how they would reconcile their family duties with politics. It was then that I realized what an equal opportunities commissioner had to do.'

After discussing the role with Wolfgang and the children, and assured of her husband's support, Marina accepted the post.

Wolfgang took time out from his studies for six months to look after the family while Marina established her new office. Within six months much was expected of her. Along with her colleague Katrin Wolf, whom she had recruited from the Peace Circle, she initiated a debate on women's rights which prompted hundreds of letters of support for the commission's work. But not everyone was pleased with her approach.

'I sensed that it was not going to be easy, but I didn't expect the resistance to my work that came from the male politicians. I wasn't going to allow their intimidation, arrogance and power-games to deter me from something I felt was most urgently needed.'

Marina pressed on with her work to obtain the views of women, and with Katrin compiled a report which provided much-needed information on the status of women in the forty-year history of the GDR.

The family unit, a nuclear version, was legally protected by a 'family code' under which women were guaranteed equality of education and opportunity. The childcare provision and the list system of election were supposed to mean that women were equally represented both in work and political life. Although the GDR had a higher proportion of women politicians than most Western countries, there was scant representation of women at the top levels of government.

'Our report was not well received because it outlined the need for changes in legislation which were required to improve the health and status of women in a society that had preached equality.

'Looking at the reports that had been hurriedly brought into my office, one of the civil servants from the Bonn Family Ministry told me that, if our report was still around after reunification [of East and West Germany], they would all be destroyed. We moved quickly to get as many as possible of the reports out to women and ministers who we thought were sympathetic to our cause, and knew that we would simply have to wait for a response.'

On 4 October 1990, after reunification, Marina and Katrin were made redundant.

They were disappointed but not entirely surprised at their dismissal but they were not about to be beaten. Armed with the report, they organized the Brandenburg Women's Week in March 1991. It was the first of its kind in eastern Germany and was a major success.

'It was a wonderful week and hundreds of women attended. We held discussion meetings, talked about the changes that were needed in government policies and held cultural events and exhibitions. It was a chance for women to be seen as being active and not passive, as many in government expected us to be.

'We had spent days and nights organizing the week and were very tired, but we also had a sense of how powerful the event had been and that something would come of it.'

Following the event, both Marina and Katrin were approached to work in the Ministry for Labour, which covered social affairs, health and women, but both declined. They had already experienced the restrictions that were sure to be placed upon them as civil servants.

In discussions that followed the Brandenburg Week, Marina knew that it would be the women who would have to bear the burden of political changes in Eastern Europe. They were the ones who were most likely to lose their jobs and have to find new ways to survive economically.

She met Katrin and together they began to plan the Ost–West Europäisches FrauenNetzwerk (OWEN), the East–West European Women's Network.

They determined that OWEN would run training-courses and workshops in women's empowerment and self-determination, would provide skills in setting up community and neighbourhood projects and self-help groups. It would also offer exchanges between women in the East and West, North and South, so that they could share and learn from one another's experiences.

Funding came from the Synod of Berlin and OWEN was established in 1991. Since its inception, it has worked with well over a thousand women from the Czech Republic, Slovakia, Poland, Yugoslavia, Russia and the Ukraine, and Marina has visited Brazil, the USA and Britain in her quest for more knowledge about the global status of women. She attended the UN Women's World Conference in China in 1995.

'In my visits I have seen poverty of unimaginable proportions, but I have also seen and met courageous and determined women who are working tirelessly at the grass roots to improve their own lives and the lives of many other people in their communities. It made me understand entirely the need for social justice that had been my grandfather's dream.

'But more importantly I also understood that, even in poverty and oppression, a person does not have to lose their self-respect and dignity.'

German reunification had profound implications for Marina's personal, as well as political, life: she was reunited with her father. He had kept in contact through letters because, although he was not a man to show his emotions, he loved his daughter and it was a joy for him to see his grandchildren. But there was always tension, which Marina only came to terms with when she visited him on his deathbed in Vienna.

'My father was a very successful and ambitious man who lived for his work. When he retired he seemed to lose all sense of direction and became very sick. I was pleased to have had the chance to spend the last few days with him.

'He was a tall and most commanding figure and I remember the times when he would visit on my birthday. My mother would sit quietly while my grandmother and my aunts attended to his needs. They admired him. He would make sparkling conversation and I think they were all in awe of him.

'I then realized how afraid I had been of him. Afraid that I would do something wrong and knowing that he wanted me to be perfect, and so I knew that he saw only my faults. I never felt that I would ever be successful enough for him to be proud of me.

'I remember one day when I was in government and he came to visit me. I had prepared coffee and we sat down in my office. In my eagerness to talk with him, I had forgotten the milk for the coffee. This he pointed out immediately, saying, "Are there no women in this place?" I jumped up straight away, as my aunts had done all those years ago, and went out to get the milk. Outside I was so angry with myself that I could have cried, and I decided that it was time for me to stop being the brave and wonderful daughter.

'When I sat with him in hospital, I no longer saw this powerful figure, but an old man who was very tired, very sick and dying. My fear went away and compassion took its place. It was a kind of reconciliation and a realization that, as a father, he had only done what he had felt able to.'

Marina continued to reflect on the past.

There were 92,000 professional spies and 170,000 informers working for the State Security Police and such was their effectiveness that organized opposition was almost impossible. Those who were identified as critics of the government were often imprisoned and sometimes tortured.

'What I have noticed is that there remains a kind of silence from people who worked for the Stasi or were very closely related to the system, and that it is harder for them to be drawn into discourse. I feel that they should have a chance to share what they feel, as victims and as perpetrators.

'We all need to understand that some of them were free to decide, but others were not. They should not just become a hidden part of our history. They too should have a voice, because I feel that maybe if they had taken another approach with me I might not have been in a position to say no.'

The expectations from most major political changes are seldom met, while the transition from the old to the new is never without its challenges.

'Life on the whole is more exhausting and I worry about my children's future. There are more opportunities, but there are also more risks.

'The pace of life is very fast; people seem to have little time for each other. In the GDR it was important for my friends and me to spend time together – it was part of everyday life. You could visit friends at any time: now you phone them before you go.

'In the GDR we were hungry to get noticed as individuals because our culture was collective, but the individualism I have come to know in the West is not the one I had expected. It is too important, too competitive, and leaves people feeling very lonely.

'I thought that in Western democracy there was more tolerance, but now I see that it is more of an indifference. A situation where you are not interested or bothered about another person, whether they live or they die.'

Marina finishes her glass of beer, picks up her jacket and makes her way out of the bar. Her work with OWEN has not always been easy, and she remembers the strain and stresses involved when the women gathered together. There were differences over practical issues which suddenly became differences between people and between cultures, and guilt and mistrust were part of a legacy of national and historical grievances. But Marina has no regrets.

'I am involved in a project called The Women's

Memory, which is encouraging women to find their own voice.

'I believe that it is important to understand and find your own way in life. I now live without a partner at my side, my two boys are independent and my two girls spend time with Wolfgang and with me. He has found a new love and she was baptized by him; and I have found a great love – he isn't a German and he is very involved in peace and reconciliation processes – and I have a circle of close friends. I think I'm a rich woman at my old age of fifty.

'I now have time to look back on my life and can understand some of the challenges I faced, and what has been most helpful in making me who I am.

'I know that I am not an object of politics or economics. I am a person.'

Malgorzata Babuchowska

6 Finding Our Voices

Revolution is often a dramatic, if not always bloody, affair which is the stuff of news reports all over the world. That was the case in Poland as the world's media relayed the birth and ultimate victory of the Solidarity movement, which overthrew the communist regime in the 1980s.

But that initial action had to be only the first in a chain of events if there were to be real changes in the social order. Not only must old laws, conventions, perceptions, life-styles and individual ways of thinking be challenged, but alternatives must also be proffered. Such work is slow, change is often incremental and the people involved will rarely, if ever, be lauded as 'heroes of the revolution'. Yet a revolution cannot truly succeed without them.

Malgorzata Babuchowska is a slender blonde woman with striking blue eyes. At first sight, she is not typical of those who involve themselves with the many challenges that emerge when a whole population face fundamental transformations in their world. In post-revolution Poland, many people are without work and bereft of a myriad of old certainties as the country moves from a command economy to the vagaries of the free market. In this social upheaval and economic strife, women's issues have dropped in the government's list of priorities but they are ones that Malgorzata continues to promote.

Unsurprisingly, it is women who have borne the brunt of the economic hardships, and Malgorzata has tried to help the women of Olszytn, her home city, as a facilitator and by using her entrepreneurial talents.

One of Olsztyn's most successful businesswomen, she applies to Women 2000, the organization she established in 1997, the same tenacity and acumen that has resulted in three thriving businesses.

Olsztyn is a small agricultural town in the Masurian Lake District of Poland. Malgorzata was born there in April 1948 and has returned there to live and work. The natural beauty of eleven lakes and a dozen or more tree-covered hills, which attracts over a million visitors a year, surrounds her home. The house is palatial, with large rooms and bohemian features, and its opulent furnishings include paintings and tapestries which are complemented by arrangements of dried flowers set on mahogany side-boards and antique cabinets. Throughout the house there are collections of fine bone china, and silver candlesticks and chalices on green marbled shelves in small recesses. Large Persian rugs and small mats with African designs cover the rich wooden floors. Healthy potted plants and African carvings stand in corners of the rooms and hall-ways. Only the piles of letters, manuscripts, folders and opened envelopes look out of place on top of the grand piano in the main reception room.

Malgorzata readily acknowledges that she has had a privileged life.

'Both my parents came from well-educated profes-sional middle-class families who were doctors, successful business people, or artists.

'My father, Tadeusz Hornziel, was chief commander of the Olsztyn Fire Brigade and my mother, Alfreda, was a nurse. I have a younger brother named Mark, who is an engineer.

'My father was a musician and graduated from the Secondary Music School in Warsaw. During the Second World War he was an urban guerrilla and a member of the underground army that constructed armoured vehicles and took part in the Warsaw Uprising, which started in August 1944. He was captured and sent to a prison camp, where he remained until it was liberated by the American Army and he was able to return to Poland. He was a noble man and did whatever he could to help anyone who was in need. I had a much closer relationship with him than I did with my mother. He was a very sociable person, and had many friends from all walks of life. In fact, he loved having people around him, and it was a very sad day when he died of a heart attack seventeen years ago.

'My mother, on the other hand, is a very quiet person and prefers to spend time alone. She gave up work to look after my brother and me. It was customary for women to remain at home until their children were at least school age, and so my mother only returned to nursing after my brother and I had started school. She was always artistic and took up painting when she retired.'

Malgorzata and her brother were brought up in a small flat which had two bedrooms, a kitchen and a bathroom; it was typical accommodation after the war, when most of the houses had been destroyed. Her mother often took Malgorzata and Mark to their grandmother's large house near the capital, Warsaw. It stood in beautiful grounds surrounded by a forest, and here her grandmother used to entertain famous artists and other guests. Many children accompanied their parents and Malgorzata enjoyed playing with them for hours in the fields; it was a very happy time for a little girl who didn't care much for school and was easily distracted by what she considered more interesting things to do.

'I had no time for school because there were lots of other things that I wanted to do when I was a child. I loved dancing and my mother said it was something I had inherited from my great-aunt Zula, who one of Poland's most famous dancers.

'In the winter I loved to go skiing and in the summer I used to swim in the lakes. Of course, I had to go to school, but I only ever did enough to get by. When it was time for exams I would spend one or two nights very quickly going over my work and only doing what I felt was needed to pass. Luckily my parents were more interested in whether I went up another class each year than in my exam results.'

Despite her lack of academic interest, Malgorzata achieved a place at Olsztyn University, where she met and married Andrzej Babuchowski. A year after they both had graduated he was offered a job in Lagos, Nigeria.

'I was very excited at the prospect of going to Africa, because I always wanted to travel. It was quite an experience, as I was very much in the minority, and I remember that the children from the village would gather round to look at me. My long blond hair particularly fascinated them and it was my first real experience of what it was like to be "different".'

That novelty wore off within a few months as Malgorzata and Andrzej settled into their new home and she began to take pleasure from the vibrancy of her surroundings, appreciating the artistry of the colourful batiks and carvings. She also became interested in the wide range of spices used in traditional African cooking, and it was this experience of new foods that gave her the idea of one day starting a small restaurant business.

When Malgorzata and Andrzej were due to leave Africa, it was difficult for them to appreciate a return home to Poland. Martial law had been imposed in December 1981 as a reaction to a demand by Solidarity, the independent trade-union movement, for a referendum to establish a non-communist government. This was followed by political and economic upheaval during which Lech Wałęsa and other Solidarity leaders were the target of periodic arrests and detentions after the movement was outlawed in October 1982.

Even though martial law was lifted in July 1983, shortly before Malgorzata and Andrzej arrived back in Poland, the continuing political uncertainty made it difficult to contemplate starting a new business.

'When the military took power, all the Western countries suspended their aid to Poland. It was then difficult to buy certain foods and medicines, and it was left to the Church to distribute a lot of these things. With such problems I knew it would be hard for me to get the equipment that I would need to start my business and, although we had to return to Poland, there was no real incentive for us to do so.'

But Malgorzata need not have worried. Their return was short-lived because Andrzej was offered a position at a university in the USA. The move proved to be a turning-point in Malgorzata's life.

'We stayed in the USA for three years and I had no idea that it would change my life in the way it did. Up to that time I was a happily married woman, I was free and could afford to travel, and I could live well. But there were many times when I wished that I could express my feelings in ways that I really wanted to and that I could share some of my personal difficulties.

'Andrzej has always been very loving and supportive, particularly in times when I was feeling isolated because I was in a different country and didn't speak the language. Even so, there were things I couldn't really share with him. Then one evening I was invited to a local women's group. I was a little apprehensive at first because I didn't know quite what to expect. I had heard about such groups but had never thought about joining one.

'I was welcomed into the group, and as we began our discussions I was amazed at how open the women were with each other. They seemed to trust each other in a way that enabled them to share very personal things. I was very conscious of some of the things I wanted to say, but still held back.

'After a little while I found the courage to speak. Everyone listened. I felt valued, and was almost moved to tears at the sisterhood that embraced me.'

In a culture that had been dominated by the repressive traits of religion and a dictatorial regime, the expression of deep emotions had been frowned upon and at times was seen as dangerously subversive. Citizens were expected to be serious and calculating rather than sympathetic and spontaneous, and there were many who, like Malgorzata, felt that the suffocating reverence for the status quo had left little opportunity for personal development.

'It was while I was in America that I realized how closed our Polish society had been, how much we laughed on the outside but that there was no real joy on the inside.

'Becoming aware of myself as a woman and knowing that I was not alone in some of my thoughts and feelings gave me a lot of strength and self-confidence, and I began to think about what I needed to do, step by step, to change my life.'

Changes were occurring not only in Malgorzata's personal life but also in the country she still loved. At the beginning of the 1980s, as well as food shortages, Poland's population had to put up with insufficient housing and the rationing of electricity. In July 1983 martial law was lifted and by 1989 Solidarity had won all but one seat in national elections; in 1990 Poland elected its first president since 1952. During that tumultuous decade, as Poland's economy crumbled, there were tentative moves by the government to allow private investment and enterprise, and Malgorzata returned home.

'I gained many ideas during my time in Nigeria and the United States, and I decided the time was right in my country for the people to try something different. I had experienced Nigerian, Mexican and Chinese food, among others, and I was comfortable with working with different spices.

'We were at the dawn of a revolution in thinking; it was a time when new ideas were going to be welcomed at last. I wanted to be involved in this new change and I wanted to make my own contribution. During the socialist era everything was under strict control. So rigid was the control over information that you needed permission from the Censorship Office to photocopy simple documents. There was a real clampdown on freedom of expression, and even events that were taking place in theatres were censored. Now all that had gone.'

Malgorzata had established two successful businesses, a food technology consultancy firm and the first of two restaurants, before her daughter, Katarzyna, was born in May 1989. Despite all the demands, she still found time to talk to some of her friends about her liberating experiences while abroad. It was difficult at first and, although her friends listened, it took some time for them to understand or see the value in sharing their personal experiences about relationships within their families or to express deeper emotions.

What Malgorzata did not realize at the time was that she had been unrealistic in expecting a rapid shift in the traditions that had led to servility and passivity within generations of women. Polish culture dictated a reticence which did not allow individuals to feel good or proud of themselves or their achievements. Although in theory women had equal access to education and work, women were collectively to know their place as wives, mothers and homemakers. They were neither affirmed nor recognized in their own right if they dared to step outside those perimeters. In a society in which citizens were supposed to surrender their individuality to the notion of a collective, personal dreams and ambitions were deemed selfish and were not to be encouraged.

Malgorzata felt strongly that there was now a chance for this to change, for women to raise their level of consciousness and realize that they had a right to self-expression. However, many barriers had first to be broken down. Malgorzata became increasingly frustrated as women resisted her appeals to share more openly with one another. None of them felt ready or able to trust others with feelings that had remained unspoken for many years. The fact that they shared many experiences made no difference at all, and eventually Malgorzata had to accept that her own heightened awareness would not necessarily inspire other women. Her enthusiasm started to wane. Then, by chance, she met an old friend who had had similar experiences.

'My friend, who was a tourist guide, told me how American visitors would compliment her on her English. She said that at first she didn't know what they were talking about, as she used to apologize a lot for not having very good English.

'It was new for her to receive compliments, because here in Poland we were not taught to think that individually we were good at something. The compliments from the tourists made her start to believe in herself and accept that her English wasn't so bad after all. This motivated her to study even more. She said she started to feel better about herself and even began to smile more than she had done in the past. It was a very simple thing but important for her.'

With renewed vigour, Malgorzata continued to talk with her friends and slowly they began to see the value in sharing, encouraging and supporting each other. Months later, a few of them began to recognize their own skills and interests and started to acquire a level of self-confidence which enabled them to try new things, while others saw the opportunity for education in a different light.

Ewa is one woman who has been influenced by Malgorzata. She says, 'I first met Malgorzata several years ago when our children attended the same pre-school. From the beginning she was a model of the extraordinary for me, a financially independent woman who ran her own business while simultaneously and assuredly joining duties of a mother and wife.

'We met at a time when I was torn apart by many personal things. My life was very difficult. I had many problems and uncertainties and they all resulted from the fact that I was not working but staying at home and bringing up my two daughters.

'I felt that time was passing me by and I was unhappy, unfulfilled and feeling unimportant. I tried to compensate for these feelings by learning foreign languages, but this was only a substitute for something I really wanted to do. Malgorzata was able to convince me that I was doing everything right and that my present activities would be of help to me in the future. Talking over my problems with her really helped, and I don't think she realized how much I appreciated the advice she gave me and how it helped to influence my decision.

'I had just started my professional activities when I found that I was expecting my third child and was more than a little heartbroken when I called Malgorzata. She was very supportive and helped me to believe in myself and my ability to manage my responsibilities at home, and continue to develop my career.

'I got to grips with myself, had my third child, mastered my English and eventually got the job I was after. Step by step I was introduced to new things in my work and I was able to take on more responsibilities. Even in times of doubt, after only a small chat with Malgorzata I was back on track. I never lost confidence once I knew that she believed in me.

'I am now working in the International Co-operation Office at the University of Warmia and Mazuria in Olsztyn. My family is happy and I have achieved harmony in my life. I feel good as a mother, a wife and a woman. I am convinced that my present feelings and the status I have achieved are due to Malgorzata, because at the right moment in my life I was able to be quite open with her and share the kinds of things I would have felt guilty about sharing before.'

Although Malgorzata herself is comfortable with the concept of feminism she was introduced to in the USA, she is acutely aware of what that word conjures up for a society still coming to terms with a true sense of equality.

'I believe that there is a difference between feminism here and feminism in other countries. In Poland, for many women feminism has a bad meaning because it suggests that women are against men. But for me feminism is not against men but about equality between men and women. If I have the same position or if I have the same degree, I don't see why I should be at a lower level or be paid less because I am a woman. In the family, I don't see why I should have to be the only one to cook and clean, if I also have a full-time job. We should share what needs to be done. I think it is silly to say women are for this and men are for that.

'I think in places like America there is another type of feminism, which suggests that some women want to be without men, but that is not generally the case in Poland.

'Many Polish men are afraid of this word "feminism". They don't know its definition but they are afraid. Some think that it is very strong women against men and that is the reason why all women's organizations are treated with suspicion. You find that women used to say, "We are not against men, we love our men." It is crazy that we have to justify and undermine ourselves in this way. I think it's fair to say that this word has negative meaning for both men and women.'

More than before, Malgorzata and some of her friends feel that it is important for women in Poland to find a voice, particularly as society and its values are rapidly changing.

'For many families it was much easier to live during the times of Solidarity than right now, because of the free-market economy, which for them is a very strange reality.'

For a country that suffered so many economic woes during the postwar socialist experiment, capitalism seemed to be the panacea. From a distance, such a system offers many rewards but it does not pretend to be equitable, and during Poland's economic transition its people became rudely acquainted with capitalism's harsher aspects. Job security became a thing of the past and many people, the majority of them women, found themselves without employment. Workplaces were no longer keen to promote women employees into middle and higher management posts; many women in such positions were abruptly replaced by men. The people who had demonstrated against the old regime and risked imprisonment, or even their lives, did so to be free from a dictatorial tyranny, but now they were faced with the tyranny of abject poverty. Many women no longer earned a wage and became reliant upon their husbands.

For many years Malgorzata had been assisting women on an individual basis, but the deteriorating situation compelled her to contemplate a more structured means of support in the form of a women's organization.

'I decided to find out about existing women's organizations which had been set up to help women in the former socialist countries. It was then that I found out about the East–West European Women's Network (OWEN) in Berlin. I accepted an invitation to one of their seminars and it was enlightening for me to know that the experiences of women, wherever they lived, were not that different.

'It was still early days for many of us in Poland to come to terms with this relatively new concept of feminism, but it was important that we learnt from women in other countries. The women in OWEN were also looking to learn from those in the West and when they invited me I gladly took part in an international exchange programme in Birmingham, England.'

The exchange programme, organized by Women Acting in Today's Society (WAITS), a grassroots community education network, introduced Malgorzata and the others to a different way of organizing women in their communities and neighbourhoods. One of the issues addressed was that of raising money for women's groups from private business sources. Until then Malgorzata had used her own finances and, although she knew it would not be easy to raise money that way in Olsztyn, it was something she considered. Upon her return home she began to plan Women 2000, which she based on the structure of WAITS. She was under no illusions about the difficulty of the task facing her and her small group of like-minded friends.

'The hardest thing was selling our idea to city council officials and their leaders, but it was important for us to have them on our side, to give us credibility and in a way to prevent them from feeling threatened. They were all very sceptical at first and they didn't trust us to make something of our organization and ourselves. After many weeks of meetings and discussions, in which we had to put forward convincing arguments for our ideas for work with women, the president of Olsztyn agreed to support us.'

Malgorzata and a few of her colleagues then began to talk with local women, introducing their ideas about the kinds of support that could be offered through the organization they proposed to create. Satisfied that she had raised enough interest, Malgorzata organized the first regional conference in Olsztyn, and it attracted senior officials from government and business as well as a large number of local women. It was a great success; the women talked about changes they wanted to see which would help them find employment, and expressed their concerns regarding the many social difficulties that had resulted from the political changes.

As in a great deal of pioneering work, considerable time and effort were required to establish and then maintain a momentum, and Malgorzata started to feel the strain, particularly when faced with the demands of her own businesses.

'When I started the organization, I didn't know how much work I was going to have to do, especially as most people were depending on me to keep it going. I simply couldn't do this alone, and so called a meeting of local women to discuss how we could go about sharing the responsibilities.

'It was a great relief when, after our discussions, I was able to sign up the twenty women needed for our constitution. Most of them were professional women who wanted to support each other as well as use their knowledge and experiences to help other women.

'We then ran a number of workshops and seminars, looking to build women's self-confidence and then encouraging women to use this confidence to make changes in their lives.'

With the aid of funds from national and international sources, Women 2000 was established as a network of women volunteers who would introduce local and disadvantaged groups of women to educational, training and business opportunities. In view of Malgorzata's own roots, one area of need on which Women 2000 decided to focus was the plight of women in rural areas, where resources were becoming scarce and life was often lonely.

'For a long time many Polish women have been denied access to positions of influence, but through networking and training we knew that we could change this. Even though it would probably take many years for this change to come, we were all committed to seeing it through.'

That commitment took Malgorzata to Olsztyn City Council to negotiate for an office for Women 2000.

'We decided that our organization, which had only volunteers, needed a base where women could get advice and be directed to places which would provide the help and sometimes the training they needed. This was the best way for us to work, because we all had very demanding jobs and could not give as much time as was required when the organization began to grow.

'We then approached the council staff who were already interested in working with women, to see if they could help us, and we were pleased when the council decided that three women should be seconded to work part-time in our office.

'They have contact with every council department and are in the best position to help women get the services they need. We also introduced them to the different organizations in the community like the Family Aid Centre, which helps women who are experiencing problems at home or suffering from depression.

'Having our office in the council means that we are at a central point for every woman in Olsztyn and have most of the resources we need. It also means that we only have to raise money to help with our training programmes and conferences.'

While Malgorzata was working and establishing Women 2000, Andrzej continued to provide much-needed support, and he is proud of what she has achieved.

'Andrzej and I have much respect for each other. He feels happy that I am doing what I really want to do and, despite his own demanding position, he will always find time to support me and the work I do with Women 2000. Men can be friends as well as husbands, and Andrzej is also my friend. We are both successful but we do not fight about positions.

'In the early days of Women 2000, there was a lot of

media interest and I was speaking on the radio and appearing in the newspapers and on television, and he said how proud he was that I was doing something I enjoyed so much. Now I am proud of him – he is a professor at the University of Warmia and Mazuria and also working with the government.'

Women 2000 is now well established, but Malgorzata still finds time to support women on an individual basis.

'Women often call me at home and if I have the time I will give whatever help I can over the phone. Sometimes, if needed, I will go out to see them and I will meet them away from their homes or away from my office. I feel that this is important so that we are not distracted. If I say I will meet for only an hour, I never go over that hour because then I am behind with my own work.

'I want to do whatever I can to help women develop all aspects of their lives, not just in business. I am happy to be in a position where I am able to help women to realize their own strength, even in times when there have been difficulties in the home.'

The communist government promoted a collectivism which has remained with Malgorzata and is intrinsic to the way she runs the larger of her two restaurants in the city. A woman of high spirits and creativity, she organizes a cabaret twice monthly. Healthy crowds look forward to these events, which often feature young artists. They are also a time for Malgorzata to don her waitress uniform and serve the customers. The money collected on cabaret nights is split: the performers receive the proceeds from the ticket sales and the restaurant has the money spent on the food and drink.

Malgorzata continues to see opportunities not only for herself but also for other people.

Ala, who has known Malgorzata for many years, says, 'There are few people who realize their dreams but Malgorzata can definitely be included in this exceptional group. She accomplishes her plans with great imagination. She concludes matters that are impossible for many people to compete with and she does it with a smile. Perhaps this is a result of the fact that she is considered reliable, trustworthy and a solid partner, not only in business but also in the everyday struggle with adversities.

'Malgorzata has been helping me and other people who were in life's troubles or so-called "blind corners". The help and support she has provided have enabled people to find work and in fact she has employed some people in her own company.

'She is always prepared to listen and, when necessary, will offer advice. Many people appreciate her openness, her entrepreneurial skills and, most of all, her courage to speak out on something when other people are silent. Malgorzata is always looking to the future with optimism and sometimes she can infect other people with this approach.

'My life has changed since I have been in contact with her. I was going through a very difficult period of my life when she helped me. She taught me how to be assertive and to look at my difficulties objectively, and I will never forget her kindness.'

Malgorzata not only believes in helping women make use of the opportunities available to them, but also, as an entrepreneur, believes they should create their own opportunities.

'A woman came to me who had been promoted in her job because the management agreed with her ideas of how she could make the company more effective and professional. Unfortunately, some of the staff did not want these changes, and instead of supporting her the management dismissed her.

'She felt they had betrayed her, and was devastated. But I told her that she could continue with her ideas and use her experience to set up her own business. She was reluctant at first and afraid that she would fail, but I worked with her on a business plan which incorporated her ideas. I was able to help her with a little finance to buy some second-hand machinery and a little place where she could start. That was five years ago. Now her business is a success and she is able to employ some members of the company that had dismissed her.'

Malgorzata reflects on her work with women in Olsztyn.

'I take great satisfaction from what my colleagues and I have achieved in Women 2000. Many women still don't believe in their own personal strength and ability to do things. But at the same time, we have helped some to think of a different way and to know that they have the potential to realize their dreams and ambitions. When we first started Women 2000, we didn't know just how much we could achieve, but through discussions and good and bad experiences we now know that we have achieved a lot.

'In America, the women gave me something that changed me, and I was able to pass this on, like a baton, to other women.

'I feel that women everywhere are the same, but we can have differences in our tradition. Africa has a different tradition, but we feel the same, motherhood is the same, our connection with men the same.

'We should be proud of who and what we are. Some women want to stay at home and their work should be valued, while other women want more satisfaction in life and they should have every opportunity to pursue their goals.

'But first you have to find yourself. I feel I have won the battle within myself and I am free to live as the whole human being that I am. For this I am grateful.'

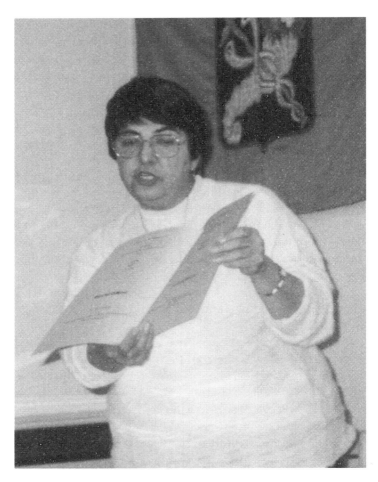

Ella Yevtushenko

7 A Future to Believe In

It has been a long and tiring morning for Ella Yevtu-shenko. The pensioner she cares for is having an afternoon nap, so Ella takes the opportunity to sit out in the small garden on a beautiful sunny day in Berlin. In the dappled shade she rests and for a short time closes her dark and expressive eyes, while her small fingers gently comb through her black hair. A smile plays on her lips as she thinks fondly of Daniel, her grandson, who lives in Canada. It is important for her to think of him, for he is her hope for the future, a good memory among the many bad ones.

Only eight years ago Ella had her own garden in the Ukraine. It was more practical than aesthetic, one where she grew the sorts of vegetables and fruit that were often in short supply in her local market.

In the years following the collapse of communism there were great shifts in the populations of the countries in Eastern Europe, as people sought to escape burgeoning and widespread poverty. In 1992, aged fifty-one, Ella joined the stream of humanity heading west to begin a new life in a united Germany.

Migration at any age is often difficult, particularly when one has to cope with a change of culture, a different language and possibly a less-than-cordial welcome. Becoming an *Ausländer* (foreigner) has been a traumatic experience for thousands of newcomers; but Ella has coped better than many, because in some ways she has been an outsider

143

all her life. At the moment of her birth she became a refugee and, for a Jew in a Gentile world, it was difficult not to
develop a sense of not belonging to the anti-Semitic society
that surrounded her.

'I was born in the Caucasus in 1941. My mother and
father, who were both doctors, had been evacuated from
the city of Kharkov as the German forces advanced. I was
only a few months old when my father was drafted into the
Soviet military as a doctor. My mother and I were then
evacuated to Uzbekistan across the Caspian Sea on a very
large ferry. My mother used to tell me that there were
many women and children packed onto the ship, on which
there was no drinking-water, in heat that was unbearable.
Many children died during that journey and their bodies
were thrown overboard. I only survived because my
mother's milk had not dried up.'

Ella and her mother, Katinka, remained in a refugee
camp for the duration of the war. Her father, Misha, paid a
brief visit during 1942 but after that his family never saw
him again. When the war was over, a friend of his visited
and told Katinka that he had looked for him without success after Misha was wounded when the hospital in which
he worked was surrounded by the German army.

It was devastating news for Katinka, who was still in her
twenties at the time. She wept bitterly, and, never losing
hope that her beloved husband might one day return, she
did not marry again.

After the war Ella and her mother returned to Kharkov,
to find that the city had been mostly reduced to rubble.
They moved into a small apartment with her grandparents
and two aunts from her mother's family. Like most of
the buildings in the city, theirs had not escaped the ravages
of war. The small rooms were dark and dreary and there
was a hole in the ceiling which made life uncomfort-
able, particularly in the winter. A small stove provided
cooking and heating and at times it was an all-consuming

preoccupation to find enough fuel to keep it working. There were very few trees left standing in the cities of postwar Ukraine.

Life was extremely difficult for almost the entire population. Food, as well as fuel, was scarce and Ella's grandmother tried to feed the family with what little flour, noodles and potatoes were available. 'When my grandmother could get onions, she would make excellent meals with them and whatever potatoes we had. She called this meal a "wrong meat dish". Although she did wonders with what little we had, unfortunately it was not enough for my grandfather, whose feet swelled because of malnutrition.'

It was not long before people started to put into place the things that made for a 'normal' existence. One of the few buildings not to have been destroyed by bombing was a school, and lessons soon resumed there. Before the war it had been a school for Jewish children, but there were to be no Jewish schools in the city after the war.

It was during her first day at school that Ella encountered prejudice.

'When I started school we had to give our father's and mother's names and our nationality – in fact, we had to give our nationality everywhere. The girl before me gave her nationality as Jewish and the whole class laughed. So when it was my turn I said, "My name is Kestenbaum, my father is away, my mother is called Yekaterina and I am Russian." I felt terrible afterwards, but it was better than being laughed at.'

After noting Ella's response the teacher asked her mother to verify what she had said, only to be told the family was, of course, Jewish. Ella was later gently reprimanded by her mother and told that denying her identity was denying herself and she must always be who she was, no matter what other people said. Even though it was a lesson Ella never forgot, she was glad to have escaped the mockery that would have come from the rest of the class.

Although she was doing what she could to settle down with her daughter and the rest of the family, Ella's mother was unable to come to terms with the fact that she would probably never see her husband again. Affected by her melancholy, her sisters, who loved her, felt that she was in desperate need of a change of environment and a chance to meet new people and suggested this to her.

After weeks of persuasion, Katinka eventually agreed to go to Moscow for a few months to stay with her brother, a lawyer, knowing that Ella would be looked after by the rest of the family. But Ella was also able to look after herself.

'My grandmother said she would look after me but sometimes, when my aunts had to go to work early and she and my grandfather were still asleep, I didn't like to disturb them. Even though I was only seven years old, I would get up quietly, make my own breakfast, wash myself, collect my things and then go to school. I also used to wash and iron my own shirts.'

Neither of her aunts had children, so Ella was the focus of their affection. Aunt Ida ensured Ella's clothes were in good repair and made regular checks that she was clear of the headlice that were rife at the time, while Aunt Zena took care of her schooling and also arranged for her to have extra tuition.

'Aunt Zena, who was a doctor, was concerned that I was to have a good all-round education and introduced me to many interesting people. She asked a friend to speak with me about the importance of my school work and to help me with my studies during the evenings after school. I liked him very much. He encouraged me to study and I remember him saying that success came from five per cent talent and ninety-five per cent hard work. At the end of our session he bought me a book which had those words in it.'

From Ella's early childhood, Aunt Ida told her that a Jew not only needed a good education to survive but also needed to be five times better than a Gentile to succeed. With these assertions echoing in her mind, the young Ella knew she had to apply herself diligently to her studies if she was to become the outstanding student her family expected her to be.

'School was everything for me and I loved my teacher. Her name was Mariya Pavlova and she was a teacher from the old days who used to wear a traditional Russian head-scarf. She encouraged all the pupils, and if someone couldn't do one thing she would suggest that they tried to do something else.'

From an assortment of female role models – after the war nearly all teachers and doctors were women – Mariya Pavlova was one of the women who impressed upon Ella how important it was to give a helping hand if it was needed.

'My teacher would also say that we should be prepared to help one another, so I started a group where girls who found mathematics or something else difficult would come to school an hour earlier and I would help them. I was good at mathematics and could explain it in a simple way so that everybody could understand.'

Ella also used the lessons from home that taught her a sense of solidarity with her peers.

'Aunt Ida used to say, "You don't have to show or speak about everything you have," so when my mother sent me exercise books from Moscow I didn't use them.

'At that time in the first and second class we had to write in the margins of newspapers because we didn't have money to buy exercise books. I thought that it was not right for me to have these exercise books when others did not.'

Despite the lack of resources and the deprivation, Ella's academic aspirations remained undiminished. Like other disadvantaged minorities, many Jewish people in the Soviet Union inculcated their children with an ambition to succeed from a very early age. Members of the majority community often perceive the resulting accomplishments, a source of pride and increased affluence within that minority group, with hostility and suspicion. Although not yet in her teens, Ella already intended to follow in her parents' footsteps and become a doctor, but she was to come up against the rigid quota system that discriminated against Jews. Only a small number of Jewish pupils were allowed to go on to university and many were prevented from studying subjects, such as humanities and journalism, which led to a profession and the accompanying salary.

Paranoia about the ethnic profile of the medical profession's elite practitioners also existed within the Kremlin, where there was a special hospital for the treatment of Communist Party members. Increasingly desperate to maintain his grip on power, in January 1953 Stalin ordered the arrest of a group of Kremlin doctors, the majority of whom were Jewish, and charged them with the murder of several Soviet leaders, including one of his henchmen, the greatly feared Andrey Zhdanov. It seemed as though Stalin was using the so-called 'Doctors' Plot' as a pretext for another of his great purges, which had exiled or killed millions of Soviet citizens in the 1930s.

'The best doctors worked in the Kremlin and most of them were Jews. It was unthinkable that they were suddenly being seen as the enemy of the people. A campaign swept throughout the country and in every establishment there were meetings on the subject. People were invited to express their "opinions" and said things like "There are many Jewish traitors and criminals amongst us." Others called for dismissals and for the Jews to be sent away, and these were demands from people who were in daily contact with Jews.'

But before any action could be taken against the Jews, on 5 March 1953 Stalin died. Ella was twelve at the time and she remembers vividly the contrast between the emotions expressed in her home and the grief that pervaded the streets outside.

'On hearing the news about Stalin, my grandfather said, "Thank God that criminal is dead." I went to school with those words swimming around in my head. The students were called together in the big school hall and our head teacher stood on a chair to make the announcement of Stalin's death, after which she fell off the chair in a faint.

'At first I was confused and wondered why my family's reaction had been so different, and then I began to think about some of the conversations and the things we did at home. One of my uncles had been sent to the gulag and I remembered him telling us how he had been tortured. He had been made to stand for days until his feet swelled up so much that his boots broke open as they questioned him. I was forbidden to speak about this outside the home or about the discussions we had about anti-Semitism.

'My grandmother secretly prayed and we celebrated in secret; we also made the unleavened bread called *matza* ourselves. I always put the holes in the bread and my grandmother baked it. On Friday evenings my grandfather would say some prayers in Hebrew, and during the Sabbath Jews would gather in a private apartment to worship. No one from the outside could see anything to do with Judaism.

'I was having to live in two worlds, a smaller one which was safe, warm and Jewish, and a much larger one which was cold and often hostile. I observed the sadness and mourning over Stalin's death at school, but I was careful to remain alone and silent.'

Even though the great purge against the Jews did not materialize, Ella was still unable to fulfil her ambition to become a doctor. An uncle suggested that she should study law, but again this profession was not open to Jews. The only way round the restriction was if someone had a relative who was a professor or if people had enough money to buy themselves into the system. Ella had neither, but this did not deter her from her studies, although she was to be denied other opportunities.

'At the age of eighteen we had final exams in every subject and our written papers were marked by outside adjudicators. If you achieved full marks you were given a gold medal and could then study without having to take further tests. I got full marks but the head teacher, who was not an anti-Semite himself, was too afraid to present me, a Jewish girl, with the gold medal. I knew that if I did well in my oral exams he would have no choice but to give me the gold medal, and so I studied very hard.

'But in the end I got only a grade four when a grade five was what I was after. I couldn't understand this, because I knew that I had answered all my questions correctly and had explained myself well.

'I later found out that my head teacher had persuaded one of my teachers to give me only a grade four in my oral, no matter how well I had done.'

She was awarded the silver medal. For many students that would have been a great success, but to Ella it was a reminder of how she had been cheated out of what she had rightfully and painstakingly achieved. It further confirmed all she had been told by her family: that Jews were often seen as second-class citizens within the Soviet Union.

By the time Ella began studying mathematics and physics at the Maxim Gorky State University of Kharkov in 1959, changes were taking place in the Soviet Union in the wake of Khrushchev's 'de-Stalinism'. Andrey Zhdanov had, before his death, begun a reign of terror in the Soviet artistic and intellectual world, but under Khrushchev a number of artists were 'rehabilitated', including the great poet Anna Akhmatova. Other poets, such as Yevtushenko, began to publish new work and there was a feeling in artistic and academic circles that there was more freedom, albeit within strict boundaries.

Ella was stimulated by a refreshing range of influences at university which helped her form a new outlook on the world. She, too, enjoyed a new freedom of expression within the intellectual debates that took place on the campus. When listening to the BBC's World Service and the Voice of America, she was inspired by the discussions of democracy and human-rights issues. Her senses heightened by so many new experiences, Ella also enjoyed falling in love and by the time she was nineteen she was married to Naum.

They had met in fifth class, at the age of thirteen, when Ella had moved school after a law had been passed outlawing single-sex schools. Ella's mother disapproved of Naum, even though he came from a comparatively well-off middle-class family; she thought they were not suited intellectually and that he would hinder her studies. It was a view shared by Ella's friends and teachers.

And yet Ella thought she loved him. Naum had pursued her ardently: he drew portraits of her and when called up to do military service he had even stolen her passport from her mother to prevent the possibility of her marrying someone else. To an unworldly young woman who had grown up in a household of women, with the exception of an aged grandfather, and whose only experience of romance was restricted to the novels she read in the ninth grade, Naum's actions were beguiling. They were both very young, and his infatuation with her led to a possessiveness which was confused with caring, and a desire which was mistaken for love. It was an ill-fated relationship from the start.

After failing the exam that would have gained him entry to the school of construction and civil engineering, Naum worked for a year as a laboratory technician. He then wanted to study to become an architect but the head of the college told him that he could not because he was a Jew. He eventually took an entrance exam for an engineering institute but failed that too. After they married and had moved into a rented room in a large house, it was left to Ella to support them both and she earned money in the evenings by tutoring after her studies at the university.

When Ella qualified as a physicist she already had a child, a boy named Misha. The rector of her university told her that her child was just one more obstacle to her getting a job, which would be difficult enough for her as a Jew and a woman. Unfortunately, the rector was right and, instead of securing work as a physicist, Ella had to be content with metal-testing in a laboratory, a job for which she was over-qualified. She did not give up hope and continued to apply for posts as a physicist while aware that, unless she could procure the support of a Party official, she would have little chance of success. But remaining in a job that was not challenging and offered no opportunities for promotion was not an option she was going to accept.

Ella's career prospects continued to look bleak until a man visited her mother, who was then working as a doctor in a children's hospital.

'The man thanked my mother for treating his grandson, who had been ill for three months. He told her that he worked on the Party's Science Committee and said that if ever she needed something she had only to ask him. My mother told him of my problems and asked if he could put in a good word for me. My rector had already written a letter saying I was one of his best students, but that would not have been enough on its own. The man responded to my mother's request, and a few weeks later I got a job as a physicist.'

However, the satisfaction she gained from her new job could not disguise the fact that for six years Ella had been in an unsatisfactory marriage – but her life was to take a dramatic turn when she went on a day-trip with a group of friends.

'With one exception, all of my friends on the trip were married and so the rest of us decided that we would try and find this friend a husband for her while we were travelling. But I was the one who found love.

'I met Valeriy on the bus. He was also a physicist and we talked for hours, until it got cold, and then he gave me his jacket to keep me warm. It was love at first sight but we were both married.' Although Valeriy and Ella vowed not to see each other again, they instinctively knew that it was going to be difficult.

For a long time, Ella realized the mistake she had made in marrying Naum. They had both been young and inexperienced; now a woman of twenty-three, she knew that she cared for Naum but that she did not love him. During one of her many sleepless nights, as her thoughts lingered on Valeriy, she decided to leave Naum.

'When I eventually told him that I was leaving and taking our son, Misha, with me, he was devastated. He visited a friend of mine and asked her to talk to me, and also pleaded with my mother. When things did not turn out he became very bitter and as compensation he demanded a room in my mother's flat, as he could not afford the room we shared by himself.'

During this acrimonious period, Ella came to see how Naum had cajoled her into marriage. He had always feared losing her and matrimony was not only his way of quelling his fear but also a means of capturing and possessing her. Inevitably, such an unbalanced relationship could not be sustained; Ella had broken free of him and was ready to begin a new life with Valeriy.

After the initial excitement of moving in with a man she truly loved, Ella's mind again returned to academic advancement. Feeling that it was important for her, as a Jewish woman, to acquire and maintain a certain status in her field, she approached her professor with regard to gaining a doctorate. The professor was reluctant to take her on and he explained that he had been unlucky: he had previously accepted two young women, who had both fallen pregnant within a year. Ella countered that she had already had a seven-year-old child and had no plans for another. The professor relented and took her on, but within months Ella was pregnant for a second time.

Sasha was born in 1971 but rather being an event of great joy it was one of consternation because he was premature.

'Sasha weighed only nine hundred grams [about 2lb] at birth, and I have often thought this may have been due to the chemicals I was working with while I was pregnant. He was a breech birth and was coloured blue because the umbilical cord had been wrapped round his neck. Valeriy was shocked. Sasha was his first child and he did not know what to do. He had not expected anything like this to happen.'

Suddenly there was tension between Ella and Valeriy; it seemed to him that she knew how best to cope while he increasingly felt inept.

'I did not cry and simply got on with what needed to be done. I drank water day and night so I could go to the hospital with my milk every day. Valeriy would say to me that I knew best and perhaps, because I had spent my life proving myself to men, I was proving to him that I did. In some ways this was a mistake because I was in control and he was not. This made him feel inadequate and I suppose I should have helped or encouraged him to do something so he did not feel so helpless. But at the time my concern was for the survival of my child and little else.'

After two months Sasha weighed two kilograms (4½lb) and was allowed to go home, where Ella diligently washed, fed and weighed him seven times a day. As time went on it became plain that the baby had other health problems; he was partially paralysed, his vision was impaired, and it was thought that his brain might have been damaged during the birth. At that time a woman was allowed two months' paid leave and then a further twelve months without pay, and it was apparent to Ella that there would be no early return to work for her.

Within six months the trauma surrounding Sasha's birth began to affect Ella. Her professor had been very supportive, and had even offered her another six months' leave should she require it and supplied her with work to do at home, but Ella felt she had to stop. Her upbringing and all the values it had infused, together with the precepts of the surrounding society, had conspired to engender feelings of guilt and shame that took her to the very edge of depression.

'I thought I could not stay at home for a year, even though Valeriy told me to, because I felt ashamed; I thought I had to work and earn money. There was a view imposed by the social system, which told me staying with my son was no value to society. My husband said nothing, but I felt guilty living off someone else's money. After the pregnancy I was very fat and needed new clothes but I felt guilty I could not buy them for myself. I felt guilty that Misha did not have his father, guilty that I had married again. I alone felt responsible for my children; I thought that I should support Misha; and that is how I think I began to lose the relationship with Valeriy, one that I was certain would have lasted for ever.'

As Sasha's health gradually improved Ella felt able to do more, and she got a job at a research institute, where she worked for the next ten years. Although the money was good, the work was undemanding and she began to look for new challenges.

'I wanted to work with young people and found out about a voluntary programme which supported the work of the police in our community. It had a number of voluntary police helpers who patrolled the streets and visited the flats; they were street social workers. I became secretary of the organization, which had hundreds of such helpers who were responsible for a new area of town which had little in the way of amenities but housed around five thousand people.

'There were meetings between the police and the public to discuss the problems in the area. The streets were without lights and there was a lot of fighting and vandalism. In the police station there was a room for youth work and another for family counselling. When there was violence in the family many women came to the station, as did some children who had learning difficulties. We also made sure to work with the teachers; today it is called open social work. It made for a busy life. Sometimes I took Sasha with me as I struggled to manage bringing up my children, my job and the voluntary work.'

Neither of her sons appreciated the voluntary aspect of Ella's work and they sometimes voiced their derision.

'My kids called my voluntary work "fools with nothing to do". They are of a generation that is much more critical: they told us we were stupid; that we had nothing of value; that they wanted to live different lives. Now Misha is a grown man he says that he thought my values a little strange but now he sees that it was another world.'

For the citizens of the USSR in the 1980s it seemed as though they were emerging into another world, one of unprecedented reform and openness. The end of Leonid Brezhnev's tenure and his eventual death in 1982 signalled the passing of a generation of Soviet leaders. Old comrades and their deputies followed him in quick succession until 1985 when Mikhail Gorbachev was made Party general secretary, at fifty-four the youngest leader since Stalin.

'As a Jew I had always experienced problems but the way the country was going under the rule of Brezhnev and his immediate successors meant that I no longer felt free to enjoy my life, as their regimes were very rigid and controlling. When Gorbachev came to power with his ideas of perestroika many people thought that he was their salvation. He became very popular when one of his first acts was to allow people to own a piece of land, plant things for themselves and build a small house.'

Although many people responded to the reforms in a positive way, others were fearful of the uncertainties that accompanied the changes. Ella and her family listened avidly to Gorbachev's speeches and became involved in the movement that looked for greater democracy.

But the movement also had a devastating effect on her family.

'I became very active in the committee for democracy. Many people had dreams of a free and open society. For me, I wanted to change a system that hounded and destroyed people as it had done to my cousin, whose only crime had been to have offered a different point of view.'

One of Ella's cousins had been thrown out of university as Brezhnev's rule came to an end because he had dared to criticize the Soviet Union's involvement in Afghanistan. He had drawn a caricature of the old leader falling from a tree after sawing through the branch he was sitting on. For this small act of defiance, the authorities harassed the cousin until he became depressed. One day, while out swimming, he drowned.

Domestically, there were also changes for Ella and her family. Sasha was now twelve but still needed a lot of attention. He was small for his age, wore thick glasses and was often picked on by other children. Everyone else in the family, including Valeriy, had argued that Sasha would have been better off in a boarding-school for the visually impaired or in a sanatorium. But Ella had persevered in caring for him.

'Everyone thought I was mad, especially when I said the best way to support my son was to resign from the research institute and become a physics teacher so that I could be employed at his school. At that time, teachers were not well thought of – in fact, they had very low status – but I had to make this sacrifice for the sake of my son.'

Invigorated by the new atmosphere of reform, Ella took the opportunity her new career provided and began to develop an innovative curriculum which would cater for the needs of individual children. Her aim was to develop not only the children's skills but also those of her fellow teachers.

'I encouraged the teachers to write their own textbooks. Ten years earlier that could not be done, and many of them were afraid. I insisted that teachers were the bridge to the next generation and after a while they came round to my way of thinking and we began to write books about teaching through teamwork.

'We stressed that, if some children were not academically inclined, we would look for the skills they had. We knew we had to look for something in every child. I knew my own son Sasha would not be an academic high-achiever but I said to him that I knew there was something that must be developed – it didn't matter what it was. There are no talentless people.

'We made sure to involve the whole community in our education work by encouraging the parents to meet us in the evenings. We particularly invited the fathers to attend, but usually it was the mothers who turned up. These were happy times for us, when we could realize new initiatives; it was a time when you could do things in your local area.'

But events taking place outside Ella's small sphere of influence led to a rapid fading of the initial euphoria. There was instability in the Baltic states, the seeds of civil war were germinating in Georgia, and in a city called Chernobyl a disaster of cataclysmic proportions was about to happen.

'My son Misha had got married shortly before the explosion at Chernobyl nuclear power station and my daughter-in-law was pregnant. We were five hundred kilometres from Chernobyl and had our windows shut. On 2 May 1986, six days after the explosion, many people were outside enjoying the lovely weather when it started to rain very hard. A short time later notices appeared in the newspapers saying that anyone who had been in the rain should undergo a radiological examination.

'A cousin of mine who was a building engineer was sent to the Chernobyl area to help with the rebuilding only ten days after the disaster. A new town was built but everyone who worked there became ill and my cousin was one of the many people who died of cancer. The new town is still deserted.'

By 1989 enthusiasm had turned to disillusionment, and not long afterwards support for Gorbachev began to wane. It had become clear to Ella and many others who were campaigning for greater democracy that maybe half the people who were on the committee with them were not in fact democrats but thinly disguised, unreconstructed *apparatchiks*.

'We lost confidence in the government when we realized that many of those in power had simply changed seats. First they were communists and then overnight they became democrats. Gorbachev had destroyed the old system but he did not build anything new to replace it. Many disappointments and hard times followed.'

Impelled by the hardships and lured by the ambitions for a better life, many of Ella's colleagues, both at work and on the committee for democracy, began to take advantage of the open borders.

'At first it was hard to understand how so many who had fought for democracy were leaving just as it looked as though it had been won. In the school where I worked, seven out of ten teachers left the country.

'Many people went to America or Israel. Jews were being welcomed because of their high levels of education and the professional status we had attained despite all the obstacles we faced. For the first time, being Jewish was seen as lucky and some people even got false papers saying they were Jewish so they could emigrate.

'My mother was in favour of us leaving but my husband asked what would happen to the country if the best people left. He also echoed his mother's words: that everyone should live and die here, no matter what.'

This divergence of views began to drive a wedge between Ella and Valeriy. He began to question Ella's inclination for always seeking out new challenges. He was a Ukrainian patriot and in his hurt he became disparaging about the loyalty of the Jews and said that they only wanted to be the best. In his anger he gave voice to his jealousy over Ella's dedication to Sasha and told her she should stop fussing and that, now the boy was eighteen, he should look after himself.

His bitterness was that of a man who had grown distant and no longer understood his wife. However, despite the increasing tension between them, when Ella eventually decided to leave the Ukraine she expected Valeriy would go with her. But when the time came he wavered and then said he would not emigrate without his mother; he knew she remained steadfast in her refusal to travel. Fate took a hand when his mother became seriously ill and made his choice to remain an inevitable one.

'It was no great surprise to me that Valeriy chose to stay. My work and study over the years, as well as the attention I had to give to Sasha, left little time for the two of us and we drifted apart.

'I was left to reflect on how and when things began to go wrong for us. Why I hadn't given enough time to our relationship and why I had taken it upon myself to care for Sasha, as if Valeriy had no part to play. But on the other hand, I also knew that I had changed, had grown stronger, and this conflicted with the woman Valeriy wanted me to be.'

Valeriy, whose father was a high-ranking military officer, was never as critical as Ella of the system. What she perceived as unjust preferential treatment for the Party elite, he viewed as just reward for faithful adherence. His view of Ella's roles and duties – that she should have stayed at home and looked after him, as his mother had looked after his father – had long been a source of contention. Just before Ella was about to leave she learnt that Valeriy had found a new love. The revelation saddened her but it was not unexpected.

'I wasn't entirely surprised at the fact that he had found someone else, and I guess that she will give him an easier life. I have loved and I have lost, but even so Valeriy remains, and will always be, my great love.'

Ella went to Israel, where many people from Kharkov had gone, but the sight of so many automatic weapons did not correspond with her ideal of a land that is safe and free.

'I didn't like to see so many weapons about the place and when a young woman got on the bus and sat next to me with a gun I made up my mind to return to Kharkov. A few days later the Gulf war broke out.'

There was little time to settle back in her home city before the attempted coup by communists in Moscow during the summer of 1991. Those who had campaigned for reform feared that it was the re-emergence of the old order and that, if the attempt to overthrow the Gorbachev government succeeded, they would be thrown into prison. Ella was advised by friends to go to Germany. She hurriedly packed a few belongings, leaving behind nearly everything except for her physics and teaching books. With her two sons and daughter-in-law, Ella travelled to Germany by car. After two days of hard driving they reached a German reception camp, where they were given a room, bedding and two days' social welfare payment. Ella's mother joined them a short time later.

'I was given 312 Deutschmarks and I was embarrassed. It was OK for my mother, who was a widow, or for Sasha, who is handicapped, but I did not want handouts because I can work. That money burnt my hands and it made me determined to work.'

Ella signed up for a language course, which was completed in ten months. A few months later she attended an education exhibition, where she decided to take a management course. The course was a mixture of theory and practice, and the practical aspect was to open a vast range of new experiences for Ella.

'I asked about work placements and although I liked the project run by the Russian immigrants, I was told I should spend my three months with a German project as this would improve my language. It was then I was offered a place with the Ost–West Europäisches FrauenNetzwerk (OWEN). I remember telling my friend about it. She was scathing and said, "Oh yes, those awful feminists who smoke a lot and hate men." Of course, when I met Marina Beyer she was nothing like that. As she spoke to me I noticed a poster behind her that said: *"If we don't help ourselves, who is going to help us?"* Those words became my motto.'

Ella's first work with OWEN was with a women's project in Moscow which promoted ways for women to help themselves and their communities. She then helped to organize a women's international conference in Kiev.

'Women came from all over the world to share experiences and to talk about the different projects they were involved with. Among many other things, it was important for me to learn that one always has to have a set of rules, whether it is in a team or a family. In our society in Kharkov there were no rules which people took for themselves, only the laws. Under totalitarianism there is no room for a person to develop a new way of thinking or working.'

As Ella listened to the experiences of other women, she realized that they were not far removed from her own. There were stories of women continually having to prove themselves in male-dominated institutions, of opportunities denied because of the suspicion that they would become pregnant, of coping alone with work and looking after the children. And she also listened as women said it was experiences such as these that had made them who they were.

'This was the first time that I realized the reality of our lives as women, and just how strong we have to be. And yet we are like the trees and can bend with different winds.

'After listening to all these stories, I began to ask myself many questions. Why are the women in Africa so responsible? Why is it that American women form neighbourhood groups? What scope do we have as women to change things?'

Ella's time at OWEN brought her into contact with a wide range of women; they have shared many experiences which have both gladdened and saddened her. Her placement with OWEN not only taught her many things about the struggles of women but also made her determined to make use of all she had learnt throughout her life.

'When I left OWEN I went to work with Russian refugees. I particularly work with young people, because I believe women are responsible for the next generation and that you cannot separate women's work and youth work. It is important that the young people have adult support and that they know someone is interested in them. When I work with youths, I have to know their parents, grandparents and teachers. Everything in this world is linked and, like a stone thrown into water, its effects are widespread.'

Ella is happy living in Germany. She endeavours to

promote better integration of Russian-speaking migrants in a newly formed intercultural society that is not always welcoming.

'I think the greatest obstacle for us in the Ukraine was the sense that we were worthless, that we could not realize an initiative on our own and that we felt that we could not change anything.

'But now we have to be healthy, open our eyes and make it easier for the next generation. We must find a new quality from everything in this world. I am always trying to activate people to make them more conscious so they can decide what they want to improve and how.

'I believe that those of us who can, must.'

Glancing at her watch, Ella gets to her feet. The sky is clouding over as she leaves the garden and goes inside. It is time to resume her work.

Abeda Davis

8 *If She should Shed a Tear*

'Our Lord! Bestow (bless) us with patience (endurance) and make our foothold stable (deep-rooted) and aid us against the disbelievers.'

Book of Baqarah: 250

Abeda Davis, a small bespectacled woman with a cheerful round face, can very often glide into a room without being noticed. When she speaks, her soft words, like her air of serenity, linger after she has gone. But the people who know her say it would be a mistake to confuse her composure with acceptance, or her gentleness with a lack of steely resolve.

With humility, she is the first to say that the part she played in the campaign against apartheid was a modest one. Abeda knows of the sacrifices countless others have made; she came into contact with many of them during her working life, and would be embarrassed if her contribution were mentioned in the same breath. And yet there had to be many women like Abeda for the crime against humanity known as 'separate development' to be brought to an end. When leading activists were taken away and incarcerated, it was left to people like Abeda to continue with their roles at a lower level, burrowing away under apartheid's edifice until its foundations were full of holes and began to crumble.

It was Abeda's work as a pre-school teacher in Eldorado Park, a mainly 'coloured' area, that led to her involvement in the campaign. 'For years I had watched and felt the pain of apartheid. I lived with it, read books about it, and I knew the history of it. I bought newspapers and followed the news, but felt that I had no real power to change anything.

'Then, when my first child started at the pre-school project, I was able to meet other women like Cecilie Palmer and Marley Fakier, to discuss what was really going on in our country. Gradually I became more aware of the courage of the men and women who were fighting to free us from the cruel clutches of apartheid, the many who had died, were imprisoned or were being hunted down by the government. That was what gave me the courage to get involved.'

The eldest of seven children, Abeda was born in Vrededorp, Johannesburg, in 1956. Her parents, children of indentured labourers who had travelled from India and Java, were very young when they were married: her mother, Ragmat Lawrence, was only sixteen and her father, Yusuf Begg, was twenty. At the time of their marriage Ragmat's father was dying and he made Yusuf promise to look after her and the rest of his family of seven children. It could have been a crushing burden, because the young Yusuf earned very little from the long, hard days at the Nugget Shoe factory that began with him getting up at four o'clock in the morning. But somehow he coped, and his unwavering kindness and consideration had a great influence on his eldest daughter.

When she was nine, Abeda's family moved to Newclare which was classified as a so-called 'coloured' area. As a small child she had felt untouched by the apartheid laws, but as she entered her teens she became increasingly aware of their inhumanity. 'I was thirteen when I began to realize that things should not be like this. My grandmother was a crippled lady and sometimes I would go with her to draw her pension. There was a bench next to the bus stop where we had to wait and it said, "Whites Only". Although she was in pain, my grandmother was not allowed to sit on that bench, and there wasn't one for someone other than white. What hurt me most was knowing that if she had sat down, even for a short time, a white person could push her to the ground or that she could even end up in prison.'

Abeda is a follower of Islam and, in keeping with Islamic custom, she is modestly clad in a long black dress which covers her from neck to ankles; it is known as a Khurta. She wears a neat black wrap round her head.

'I used to wear fashionable clothes but after I had a major operation in 1995, I decided that I would give myself to Islam and do the correct thing. I had grown spiritually and it was like a new beginning for me.'

Abeda's faith helped her to cope with the trauma of South Africa's rigid laws of segregation.

'I was taught by my religion that, no matter what the law of the country said about segregation, in Islam there is none and so I was able to look at people as people and not judge them on the basis of their colour. What was preached in Saudi Arabia, in Mecca, was not what was being taught in places like America, where it was said that you should hate the white man or not show kindness to anyone other than another black person.'

Abeda's schooldays were memorable ones at the Coronation Ville High School, a so-called coloured school, where she was a bright student and also excelled at athletics and hockey.

'I was active in my youth playing sport, and used to question why we could not play a match against a white team. I always believed that we were as good as the white teams, even with poorer facilities, but it was simply not allowed.'

Travelling to athletic meetings and hockey tournaments provided relief from some of the restrictions on her at home.

'Although many of my friends went to clubs and discos, I was never allowed to. As a teenager, there is always an excitement about doing something you know that your parents would not approve of, so when I went away to compete I took the chance to go to a club.

'Throughout the tournament I kept thinking about the evening when I would have a taste of what everyone said I had been missing. When I walked into the club I was excited and immediately soaked up the convivial atmosphere with the dim coloured lights and the music. But things went downhill from there. The music was too loud, I couldn't dance and felt out of place.

'My friends were keen to impress upon me all that they had been talking about and made sure to include me in everything they did. I was grateful and, although I didn't really enjoy it as much as I thought I would have done, I was glad to have had the experience.'

The parental restrictions on Abeda and her brothers and sisters, which included what and where they could and could not eat, did not worry them too much. To them, they were being brought up in the way their parents considered the best.

'This was something we understood and respected. For example, on Fridays when we came home from school we were expected to go to the mosque, and we did. After a little while, it wasn't a matter of anyone telling us to go, it simply became a part of our lives.'

When Abeda left school, she wanted to go to teacher-training college but there was no money to support her and so she had to find a job. She worked in the offices of elite stores like Edgars and Foschini, where she was responsible for stock-taking. The clientele were invariably white, as were the supervisors and managers. As a so-called coloured woman, she felt that her position was always under threat if she ever stepped out of line. There was an unwritten rule that, no matter how badly she and others like her were treated, nothing would be done about it. Like many other so-called coloureds, Abeda did not challenge the uneasy working environment. Instead, she bided her time until she was able to find a job with better working conditions and a place with values similar to her own.

This opportunity came when she was employed as a switchboard operator at a local clinic.

'At the Park Lane Clinic I began to see that there were better ways for people to relate and work with each other. Our office was racially mixed and I saw what little was required for people to treat each other with dignity and respect. I also understood that when people fell in love they forgot about colour, even though it was dangerous because of the Immorality Act. Such relationships had to be hushed up and some people left the country, simply because they wanted to be together. A cousin of mine who married a German had to leave South Africa in the 1970s or they would both have been thrown into prison.

'I enjoyed working in a mixed team. Muslims, Jews, Christians and others, black and white, side by side. I was able to get on with everyone. My parents had impressed upon us the word "Saber"; it means "tolerance"and was a big word in our home.'

Abeda met and married her husband, Jasien, in 1977. She did not work again until 1984, when her first child was four years old. With the demands of a young family, she could only observe the apartheid regime in a painful silence, relying on her faith and spiritual beliefs to enable her and her family to endure the barrage of injustices that rained down on them. She did not know that she was soon to join the growing number of women who were becoming political activists.

'I met Marley Fakier when I enrolled my daughter, Tayeba, at the pre-school project she had started. Marley was an ex-teacher who had been thrown out of teaching by the education authorities because she was a political activist.

'One morning when I arrived at the pre-school, I could see that they were having some difficulties with the children. Marley was in hospital, and there were only two people, an appointed teacher and Marley's husband, attending to the children. I offered to help and continued to do so for a number of weeks.

'When Marley returned, she asked me to stay on. It was an honour for me to be working with someone like Marley. I received training from her and talking with her made me realize that I could contribute towards our country's liberation.

'Before this time I had not thought about work with women, and Marley's desire to uplift women was one of the factors that I admired in her. She helped me to realize that I had something to offer outside my home and family and I was inspired by the way she was always looking to empower women.'

Within a few months, Abeda and a number of other women whose children attended the pre-school project joined the African National Congress (ANC). When it was banned they joined the United Democratic Front (UDF) and later on the Federation of Transvaal Women (Fedtraw).

Three years later a silent and frustrating period of Abeda's life came to an end, when she found herself, with like-minded women, in the heart of the struggle. She recalls with emotion her involvement in a Women's Day demonstration at Wits University. 'I was with a group of around thirty women from Eldorado Park. We divided ourselves into smaller groups of three or four and were posted at different strategic points. Me, three other women and our children stood in a valley.

'At first I was ecstatic. It was like a dream that I was out there with hundreds of other people, making my stand against apartheid. But when I saw a number of armoured vehicles and police cars racing to where people were, that feeling changed and I started to feel afraid.'

Gunshots rang out and people scattered as the armoured vehicles moved in. One woman, who had gathered her children round her, suggested to Abeda that she and her children should take cover in a nearby marquee in case the police started to shoot. It was only then that she fully realized the danger.

'My first thought was for the safety of my children, and then I thought about what I would do if anything happened to them. I rushed into the marquee and held my children close to me. I was angry with myself for having exposed them to what I should have known would be a dangerous situation.

'But as women we had decided to take our children with us because it was important for them to know what we were struggling for. I had with me my two daughters, Tayeba, who was seven years old, and Kaamila, who was five, and my son, Nizaam, who was three. Our strong feeling was that our children should be able to understand what we were struggling for and should become part of that struggle.

'Imagine that you are walking past a park with your children and all the white children are on the swings and the seesaw and they ask, "Mum, why can't we go and play?" You have no answer because there really isn't one that would be sufficient. These were the thoughts that occupied our minds.'

There were no casualties among the women and children, and Abeda was not put off taking her children to other demonstrations. But she went alone to ones she felt might erupt in violence on account of police brutality.

Strengthened by her frontline experiences, Abeda continued to play her part in the struggle by attending political meetings, distributing leaflets and taking messages to people who were in hiding. She was also the driver for the pre-school bus and, while driving around the neighbourhood to pick up the children, she would note where the roads were blocked and places where the police were standing guard. This information was then disseminated throughout the network of activists.

Abeda had been warned about the possibility of being followed by the security police, but kept diligently to her task with plans of her own.

'I would make a point of taking a certain route every other day. One day, when I went for the bus to start my round of pick-ups, I saw a car parked near the school building, with two men sitting in the front. When I drove off it followed and it continued to do so as I stopped at each pick-up spot.

'I always enjoyed watching thriller movies and so kept checking in my rear-view mirror as people did in those films when they thought they were being followed. It never occurred to me at the time how silly it was for me to try and give them the slip, but I just had an urge to do so and turned quickly into a street where there was a post office, way off my normal route.

'Needless to say they were much more experienced than me and I didn't manage to lose them.'

Not knowing what might happen to her, but fearing that she would be ordered to pull over and be questioned, Abeda was worried about the children in the bus and how they might be affected. Although she knew she had to remain calm, she was also very nervous, and thoughts of home and family flooded her mind.

'My husband was always aware of the situation in our country but he was not involved in any political way and feared for my safety. At times he used to say that one day the police would take me and the children away and then he would not know what to do.

'When my children sang political songs he would

caution them and explain the dangers of them being heard. He always expressed his concern when I was going to political activities but he never tried to stop me; and I noticed the relief on his face when I returned home. If ever anyone spoke against my involvement in the struggle, he supported me, saying that I was doing something I felt was important for me and for the future of our children. I appreciated his support.'

When Abeda parked outside the pre-school building, the car also pulled up and stopped a few metres behind her. She ushered the children into the building and, a little shaken, told Marley what had happened. Having had similar experiences, Marley was able to reassure her, suggesting that it was a crude attempt at intimidation rather than anything worse. Both women remained in the building until the car eventually drove away.

'I was relieved they had gone, because this was 1986, a very violent time in our history. Many activists were picked up by the security police and thrown into prison without reason. The government was so afraid of what these activists might do that they preferred to empty the prisons of "ordinary inmates" to make sure there was enough room for them. It was hard to believe that they would rather have murderers on the streets than activists.

'Fortunately, I was never arrested and only really played a very small part. My mother was afraid for me in case I got picked up. Neither she nor my father wanted to be involved themselves and they didn't think much about the various organizations that were part of the struggle. In fact she sometimes said, "If anything happens to you don't think that the C & A will be able to help you." She really meant the ANC, of course.'

Abeda took part in rallies and marches against apartheid, and also fought on other levels. She campaigned with others when the government tried to make Eldorado Park, Johannesburg, autonomous, which would have led to

higher rents and devolved responsibilities for environ-
mental development and upkeep at inflated costs. She
worked at the local advice centre and campaigned for fairer
rents. She also helped to provide homes for people who
were uprooted from other areas and dumped in Eldorado
Park as a consequence of the 1950 Group Areas Act, which
dictated where the different races might live and work.

'We worked with the Red Cross, providing blankets
and food and putting up tents for up to twenty families,
including children. We had to deal with children who
came from broken homes and deprived backgrounds. We
fought for decent homes and were eventually given houses
in Extension Ten in Eldorado Park.'

Abeda did not achieve her ambition to become a fully
qualified teacher, but her pre-school teaching brought her
much satisfaction.

'I did not attend any college or course on pre-school
education but received on-the-job training from Marley,
attended lectures wherever I could and read about and did
some research on the development of children. I think that
my love for the work inspired me to learn as much as I
could on the subject.'

The success of the pre-school programme brought
recognition from a number of agencies, including Fedtraw,
who approached Marley to spread the project throughout
Soweto. As pre-school co-ordinator, Abeda worked with
Marley to train other co-ordinators as the schools
expanded. This development also provided jobs for
mothers who trained to become co-ordinators.

'One of the first places we were to set up a pre-school
project was in Heavenly Valley, a place where people had
been moved to from the city.

'This was in the 1980s when so many places were taken
away from black and so-called coloured people and were
given to whites. Places like Alberts Row, Sophiatown and
District Six in Cape Town. Most people had to leave their

belongings behind and were made to live in shacks. When parents turned up with their children, we also gave them food and clothes.

'A Professor Whisson, of the Rhodes University in the Eastern Cape, was employed by our funders to evaluate the project. His report stated that the curriculum was the best in the country because of its non-racist and non-sexist approach, and recommended that a pre-school training institute be established in order to make it more widely available.'

The Institute Thuthuka, which is Zulu and means 'rise up', was established in 1994 and Abeda was responsible for delivering training in pre-school education on a national scale. It ran successfully for two years but had to close down when the funding stopped.

'That was a terrible time for all of us and we were devastated. All finances that had been coming from overseas through the European Union were frozen due to an organization's misappropriation of funds that should have gone to poor children.

'It was grossly unfair that we were being penalized for someone else's dishonesty and misdemeanour. We tried to explain to those in charge the value of our work and that we could prove how well we accounted for all the money we had received, but they were not in a position to listen or help us and so closed us down.

'Sadly, we were left only to reflect on the satisfaction we felt having been able to provide stimulating activities for hundreds of children who would otherwise have been denied these opportunities because of the high costs of day-care and crèche facilities.'

As well as benefiting the children, the pre-school project had enabled their mothers to acquire a level of political awareness that had galvanized some of them into action against apartheid. With the ending of apartheid and the closure of the Institute, Abeda, whose skills as a trainer had been recognized by many people, began working with the Women's Institute for Leadership Development and Democracy (WILDD). She developed programmes for women who wanted political involvement in South Africa's new democracy and were seeking positions in government.

'At this time Marley and Cecilie [Palmer] were planning the Women's Democracy Programme under WILDD and I had responsibilities to develop it. I missed working with the children but welcomed what was a new challenge for me.'

Abeda's versatility was also utilized in other areas of WILDD's work.

'Mothers who had been taking their children to the pre-school project also talked about problems they were having at home and so I trained as a counsellor and worked with Women Against Women's Abuse (WAWA), which was set up to help women who were experiencing domestic violence.

'This was quite a shift for me and one that taught me a lot about the suffering of women on a scale I could not even have imagined. Sometimes, when women cried as they talked about the cruelty they were experiencing, I found myself crying with them. Other times I listened and helped them to understand that they had choices.'

Gina Matemane, a tall, thin woman with a pleasant voice, arranges the pots and pans on a shelf in the kitchen of her small house. She then sits on the chair she has pulled out from under the table and recalls her first session with Abeda.

'When I went to WAWA, I was at my wits' end and just didn't know where or who to turn to. The fact that Abeda said to me that she would do everything she could to help me put my life back together again gave me hope. She sat and listened to me and I wasn't afraid to tell her how bad things were at home. Speaking to her helped to ease the pain and distress I had been experiencing for a long time and I could see that there was light at the end of the tunnel. I feel much stronger now with the counselling she has provided and, although I am still trying to sort out my problems, I know there is someone out there fighting for me. As long as Abeda doesn't give up on me, I will not give up hope.'

While financial constraints are a main obstacle for some women wishing to leave violent relationships, they are often also the cause of it. Unemployment and little money, which barely covers basic needs, give rise to tension and discontent in families. If a husband is lucky enough to have work, he is sometimes reluctant to give his wife enough money to support her and the children, preferring instead to spend it on other women, alcohol or drugs. Some men even refuse to pay maintenance, leaving women to struggle on a pittance to feed and clothe their children.

Abeda is resolute about what she has to do.

'There continues to be a prevailing myth that women must obey their husband and must always make him feel like a man. Men exploit and exert this power and believe that they have the right to beat up their wives.

'Many women are not aware of their rights and furthermore are not always assertive enough to exercise them. We have to help women realize the power they have to change the course of their lives and that they don't have to put up with abuse.'

For Abeda and many others, the ending of apartheid did not bring the benefits they had hoped for. They believe that the disappointment would not have been so great had there been more jobs, better housing and improved health services. The dire circumstances have led to some people taking to other means to satisfy their needs.

'In our area crime has increased and corruption has escalated tremendously. It is no longer safe to walk in some places.

'In the days of apartheid we had street and crime committees which were vigilant and kept crime down to a minimum. We had a greater purpose; now there is no purpose. It's almost as though there is an apathy that says we have nothing to fight for any more.

'My grandmother is now able to sit on a bench [at the bus stop] but there is a new frustration, one that exists because there are no jobs. This leads to more violence, and women and children are being abused as a way for men to vent their frustrations.

'More women are having to work and this causes resentment among men, who try to put them down with disparaging remarks like "So now you think that you are wearing the pants." '

Abeda herself is aware of the effects of unemployment. She became the breadwinner when her husband, Jasien, was made redundant by the factory where he had worked for twenty years, a devastating blow.

'Jasien and I have a very good marriage. We still love each other very much and are the best of friends. He has always been my rock. When he was made unemployed, I had to be his. I constantly encouraged him and assured him that something would come up.

'To suddenly find himself as a house-husband was very tough on him. He had never been unemployed since the age of sixteen and I noticed the change in him. It was from someone who had always been dependable, friendly, even-tempered and loved joking, to someone who was serious, frustrated and sometimes distant.

'He could not bear it that I had to carry our financial burden alone. The worst was that I had to leave for work early in the morning while he could still sleep, so he began to get up even earlier to make coffee for everybody and drove the children to school. He kept himself busy by fixing everything in and around the house and learnt how to cook.

'There was a time when he seemed to have been speaking with everybody in Johannesburg and visiting every

factory in his search for work, but there was no work, and
to make matters worse other factories were also closing
down. It was hard for us and the family, and I remember
having to count every penny he got from his redundancy
package and my salary.'

While Jasien was out of work, the couple performed the
hajj, the pilgrimage to Mecca, prescribed for every Muslim
once in their life, provided they can afford it. (The pil-
grims' principal activities are walking seven times round
the Ka'bah holy shrine, kissing and touching the Black
Stone; and climbing two local hills, Mount Safa and Mount
Marwah, seven times.) They had to use a lot of Jasien's
severance pay, but felt sure it was worth it. They had much
preparation to do, and Abeda felt this played its part in
helping Jasien through his personal struggle.

'When we were there it was like stepping into a different
world, one of togetherness and peace. If I never understood Islam before, I certainly understood it when I was
there. We had saved long and hard to fulfil this obligation,
but it was money well spent. It was a time of great importance to us because we knew it was a once-in-a-lifetime
experience – we would never have enough money to visit
again.'

On their return from Mecca, Jasien found part-time
work, and a number of temporary jobs followed; he continues to hope for permanent work.

With WAWA fully established, Abeda and Marley were
asked by government agencies to run group meetings to
debate draft papers on proposed government legislation
known as the Muslim Personal Laws.

In Islam, men are allowed to marry more than one wife.
The Qur'an specifies that they can only take another wife
(up to seven in all) if they can do justice to them, treating
all their wives equally without having a favourite or
showing favour to a particular one.

'The men do not think this out clearly before they marry

their second or third wife. It is impossible to feel the same affection, give equal time, money and attention to more than one person. There are also conditions spelt out in the Qur'an that state when a second wife can be taken, but they are often ignored. Very often lust is the simple reason for a man to take another wife.

'Men cannot simply divorce their wives to get married to younger or more beautiful women without real cause, but they do. They often get married to women in different areas without the knowledge of their current wives, and some receive divorce papers without being informed by the husband of his intentions. Whatever happens, the women stand to lose out on every level and so something must be done.

'This is what we shall be debating. A fair chance of happiness and a better quality of life for Muslim women in South Africa.'

As she sums up her hopes and worries about the future, Abeda once again focuses on her faith and how it has kept her whole.

'Muslims pray five times a day. A prayer before dawn, a prayer when the sun has passed the zenith, a prayer in the late afternoon, one when the sun has just set and the night prayer when it is completely dark. The dawn, sunset and night prayers are not a problem, but due to my work it is not possible to perform my other two prayers on time. It is permissible to do it when you have the time or as soon as possible, so I do them just after I have said my sunset prayer.

'It is not easy to uphold your prayers when you work, but it is our way of life and in those dark days of apartheid they gave me the strength to do what I had to do, and continue to do so now.'

Abeda thinks about her children, Tayeba, who is now twenty, Kaamila, eighteen, Nizaam, sixteen, and Asqilla, thirteen.

'My hope for their futures is that the experiences they had and the examples and teachings we have passed to them will make them strong, competent adults who will live an Islamic life and always care for their fellow human beings.

'They have strong characters and sometimes I fear that they are a bit too strong-willed. I also fear for their safety in these crime-ridden times.

'I do regret that, due to lack of money, we could not manage to send them to college or to further their studies, after completing matric. The job opportunities are limited for them and they too cannot find employment. Nevertheless, I do not doubt that they will succeed in life *insha-Allah* [God willing].'

As South Africa ventures into a new millennium, and despite the high crime rates, Abeda remains optimistic.

'I always believe that there is hope. I also believe that if we were to look at the lives of women, and the love we have inside of us, in spite of all our hardships, we would understand that God has put a woman on such a high pedestal that whosoever causes her to shed a tear will not be looked upon favourably.

'This is my message to our society.'

It is obvious that in all Abeda's actions there is love of her fellow human beings and of her Islamic faith. And, like many people who have a great faith, she is content for her actions to set an example to others.

The wrongs of the apartheid regime will take many years, perhaps many generations, to put right. Equality and justice, in a material sense, for many millions in South Africa seem as far away as ever. Indeed, in August 2000 President Thabo Mbeki launched an attack on the growing inequalities in his country and echoed the view of many activists, including Abeda, when he expressed his contempt for 'a value system based on the pursuit of personal wealth at all costs'.

How he addresses those inequalities only time will tell. But as South Africa marches towards globalization and a free-market economy, it is certain that many of the country's poorest workers are at risk of losing their jobs.

No doubt a disproportionate amount of the resulting poverty will impact on the women of South Africa. But there will always be women ready to help and to share whatever they have. Most of what will be shared cannot be measured in financial or material terms; time, knowledge and a spirituality that transcends religion and race. Abeda is one woman who will continue to be ready to share, as she does with one of her favourite prayers, which she has found most useful when in need of the strength to continue with her work.

Vesta Smith

9 A Journey through the Shadows

A row of blue and white hoops, made from old worn-out tyres, rises from the dusty dirt sidewalk and a group of listless young men loiter on the corner of the street. They aimlessly shuffle their feet in the dry red-brown earth and pay little heed to the old woman who weaves her way through them on a warm autumn day in Soweto. The small, round, energetic figure makes her way to her red-brick house across the road as the young men are distracted by the arrival of a battered old Ford car which has music blaring from its open windows. They know her as Vesta Smith, a so-called 'coloured' because of her light-brown skin. Some of them may have a dim notion that she played her part in the 'liberation struggle', but they are too pre-occupied with the struggles of everyday life in the township to give it much thought. They do not see her close the door behind her.

Like most of the houses in the Noordgesig district, Vesta's home has a metal roof and is hemmed in by an ornate brick wall and iron gate. Compared to the house in Winter Street to which she moved in 1941 with her mother and three sisters, her present home may seem luxurious: it has two bedrooms, a living-room, a small kitchen, a bathroom, running water and electricity. The old house in Winter Street had only a steep corrugated-tin roof, bare walls of brick and mortar and a dirt floor made level with cow dung. Her family, the Palmers, had been forced out of their own home in 11th Street in the Fitas area of Johannesburg, under the Group Areas Act, an act passed in 1950 to assign the different races of South Africa to separate areas. Although Clara Palmer had tried to be strong for her daughters, she could not hide her sadness and worries about the future from Vesta, who was then a young woman of nineteen. Hard choices had to be made about what possessions would fit into the much smaller house in Soweto that the government had allocated to them, and most of the family's larger pieces of furniture, including a treasured piano, were left behind.

Vesta settles into one of her comfortable armchairs and removes her spectacles to wipe her eyes before replacing them to gaze at the pictures on the walls of her living-room. Images of five generations of her family adorn the walls and next to the tall wooden display cabinets are photographs of her old friends Nelson Mandela and Walter Sisulu. In a corner stands a piano.

The car at the junction moves away, the noise of the music fades into the distance and Vesta Smith begins her story.

'I was born on 20 July 1922, the third of five children. My mother's name was Clara and my father was Stephen Palmer. He was a slim, dark-skinned man who died of tuberculosis at the age of forty-three when I was only five years old.

'I have only a vague memory of my father, although sometimes I am surprised at how clear the picture is, and I do remember some of things he did. He was a clerk at the Robinson Deep Mines on Eloff Street, and my mother was a seamstress and also a washerwoman who did washing for the households of the white men my father worked with. The whites lived in another part of the complex. They had big houses, of course, with electricity and everything.

'We lived at the other end of the complex; there was no electricity and sometimes it was so dark that we would end up at other people's houses when trying to find our way home. We had to put up our own houses. Today, people might call them shacks but to us they were not shacks. Our family had a large piece of ground where my father was able to put up a big house with three bedrooms, a living-room and a lounge. Everything was big and spacious. The walls and roof were made of corrugated iron and the floor was made of wooden planks. As we were next to the compound, where thousands of miners lived, I think they helped my father to build this house. Although the land was provided for free, my father later bought himself a plot of land in a place called Newclare, where he had cattle, and built another house. I think it was a provision for his old age or in case he should lose his job at the mine; if that happened, we would have had to leave that house and find another place. So I suppose you could say the second house was a kind of insurance.'

The Palmer family was never to live in Newclare. Following Stephen's death, the manager of the mine announced to everyone that Clara Palmer and her children would always have a home within the complex. But when the manager died people around the mine began to make life unpleasant by openly questioning what right the Palmers had to stay there when they did not even have a family member working for the company. It was then that the family relocated from Eloff Street to Fitas; their last move before Soweto.

Although Vesta did not find out until many years after his death, her father had in 1912 been a founding member of the ANC (then called the South African Native National Congress). The Palmer house had been used as a meeting-place and men such as Dr Mulema from Botswana, Bud Mbelle from Pretoria and Sol Plaatje were regular callers. Her mother, Clara, was not politically inclined and was reluctant to tell her daughters about their father's involvement in the ANC, even though Vesta's godfather was Kgosi Montsiwa who was one of the ANC's leading lights at that time.

Life for the Palmer girls was relatively privileged because of their parents' insistence that they receive a good education. Such encouragement was unusual at that time, as poorer young women could expect little more than to become wives and mothers; while those who were slightly better off and educated could set their sights on careers in professions such as nursing or teaching.

'Because of where we lived in town we had to walk four miles to school and four miles back. The school was in the centre of Johannesburg and it was called the Albert Street School. It was a Methodist school. In fact, in those days nearly all schools were attached to a particular Church. I stayed at Albert Street until I reached standard six at the age of thirteen. I then went to Pretoria to a Methodist institution where I did a teacher's training course for three years. My eldest sister, Mercy, went to St Peter's, one of the best schools in South Africa. The one after me, Toy, decided at standard six that she wasn't the book type and chose to go to work. The baby, Esme, went to a school that was called the Euro-African, a so-called 'coloured institution'. My sister Bubbles, who would have been two years older than me, died when she was five.'

Vesta enjoyed her schooldays and was fond of sport, especially hockey, much to her mother's disapproval. Clara Palmer was a protective mother and was always worried that a stick would injure her daughter's legs or that a ball would hit her in the face. Every Tuesday and Thursday there was hockey practice and on those days Clara would go to meet her daughter to check that she was all right, scold her, and then try to deter her from taking part in such a dangerous sport – with the strap she was carrying! But, despite the scolding and the hidings, Vesta continued to play hockey until she went to college.

Boys also featured in Vesta's early life. There were two

types: the boys who attended the elite St Peter's School and the young men from the northern province, whom the locals called the 'Amalaita' . The latter were looked upon as gangsters, not because of any criminal intent or activity, but because of their wild dancing in the streets, accompanied by loud, shrill whistles which disconcerted and sometimes intimidated the locals.

'One night some of the boys from St Peter's were escorting a group of us girls home from the cinema when the Amalaita appeared. The boys from St Peter's turned and shouted: "Oh no, they are coming after us!" and with that ran away, leaving us behind. We got home without bother and learnt that night that the Amalaita were not gangsters and that some of the boys from St Peter's were not as brave as they had led us to believe.'

Vesta was an outstanding student and the principal of her school told her mother that she would make a very good teacher and recommended that she train as a teacher. Clara Palmer was proud of her daughter's achievements, and encouraged and supported her throughout her training. Once the three-year course was completed, Vesta taught for a few months at her old school in Albert Street, but found that she had neither the patience nor the inclination to continue with teaching as a career.

'I left and went to work in a lampshade factory and then I went into the Allied Workers Union as a typist. It was that involvement that made me aware of what was really going on in South Africa. What I learnt from the trade union was that I am a person in my own right, so I don't have to say "Boss" or "Madam" to anyone. This was a revelation, for as a family we had been brought up to believe that the white man ruled. That was really down to my mother, who was an admirer of the British royal family. When the Duke of Windsor came along to the Rand Club, a place for society's white elite, in Loveday Street, we were made to dress in our Sunday best and my mother, my sisters and me stood for hours watching the prince going back and forth. In 1947, King George VI, Queen Elizabeth and their two daughters paid a visit to South Africa that included a motorcade through the streets of Soweto. Again, my mother wanted us to join the throng who lined the streets, but this time I was much older and refused. They may have been the King and Queen of England, but they were not my King and Queen. My mother was angry and told me that I was stubborn and a rebel. It was a good while before she spoke to me again.'

It was in that year, 1947, that Vesta joined the Johannesburg City Council. She joined as a secretary but the job eventually turned into something similar to social work. She became involved with old-age and disability pensions and services, as well as housing issues. With the onset of the Apartheid Laws from 1948, she saw at first hand their devastating impact on individuals and families, and became an anti-apartheid activist.

'In 1956 I joined the ANC Women's League when they arranged the big march to Pretoria against the Pass Laws. The laws were intended to control the movement and rights of residence of African men, particularly those in urban areas. Our men were being oppressed by these laws; at certain times they could not be on the streets, and every time a policeman met them they had to produce a pass or risk a fine or imprisonment. When the Pass Laws were being extended to African women, we decided to fight it. As women we were saying "No". It was a great day, with almost two thousand women led by Lilian Ngoyi, who was president of the Federation of South African Women. We carried placards and were united against laws which wanted to control the rights of African women to live and work in urban areas or even to be with their husbands and families in the townships. Although the march was not successful by way of getting the laws repealed, they were not so rigorously enforced on women after our protest.'

At that time, Vesta was not a paid-up member of the ANC but she allowed her house to be used as a meeting-place for women who were banned, such as Helen Joseph and Albertina Sisulu. She had been friends with Albertina's husband, Walter, for years and had first met him as a trade unionist. She also knew Nelson Mandela and Oliver Tambo, who were in partnership in a law firm in Johannesburg.

'In those days, very few people in Soweto had cars and often Nelson would stop on the road and give people a lift. He was always an open and warm-hearted man. In my view Walter and Nelson never tried to persuade anyone to join the ANC. They simply talked about what was happening in South Africa and about their work. It was more about them saying, "The choice is yours." I took the choice and supported the ANC in any way that I could, but I never became a card-carrying member. It wasn't until the leaders returned from exile that I officially joined up.'

Often it was more useful if activists were not paid-up members of any organization that was seeking change in South Africa, as the government was banning them so regularly. When the ANC Women's League was outlawed the Black Women's Federation was created to take its place. That body was then split and organized on provincial lines and Vesta became vice-chair of the Federation of Transvaal Women (Fedtraw).

Although she found her political work time-consuming, she felt a duty to confront the injustices that surrounded her and to a certain extent her work at the council enabled her to do that. It was fulfilling until the doctrine of apartheid began to influence the department in which she worked.

'I worked in the department for almost eighteen years but left when the heads of department were instructed to carry out the policy of the national government. Until then we were all together, people of different races, working side by side, but when they introduced the Black and Coloured Sections and the Indian Division, I just couldn't take it. People changed. It was as though we could no longer trust each other. Apartheid had made our department a very unhappy place.'

Vesta resigned. She worked at the head office of Edgars Stores for three years before securing a job with the South African Council of Churches (SACC). During the seventies the SACC was one of the main opponents to apartheid and Vesta became involved in providing support for the families of people who were imprisoned or in exile. She applied herself diligently to her task for seven years until one morning she arrived at her desk to find a pay cheque and a curt note that informed her that she was dismissed. Bewildered, and unable to find anyone who would give her an explanation of why she was no longer required, Vesta collected her belongings and left. (It was some years before she found out what lay behind her dismissal.) As she left the SACC's office she had no inkling that her own family would soon be in need of the kind of support she had provided for so many people during the previous seven years.

In 1975 Vesta began to work for the South African Committee for Higher Education Department (SACHED), which was a non-governmental organization set up to assist those who had gone through the Bantu education system.

'The Bantu education was enforced in the early fifties. Until then, education was education – it didn't matter whether you went to a black school or a so-called coloured school or even a white school, the end product was you all sat the same exams. But in 1953, Hendrik Verwoerd, minister of native affairs, who was later to become prime minister, pronounced that a black person need only be taught to carry water or chop wood. That is when they separated education and introduced apartheid into the schools.'

The seeds sown by the Bantu education system began to reap a grim harvest in the summer of 1975, when African students refused to be taught in the language of the Afrikaner. The students' protest was cruelly suppressed by the state and in just ten days, according to the government, 176 were killed and more than a thousand were wounded, though the black organizations put the figures much higher. The students' actions continued for another four months, leaving thousands more casualties.

At the height of the protest, Vesta, who had by now become a respected figure, was asked to address the students at Bosmont High School, in an attempt to bring calm to a highly volatile situation. Upon hearing that there had been a number of casualties, Vesta decided to go to the cathedral to find Bishop Desmond Tutu, to whom she felt the students would listen, but he was away from Johannesburg. Feeling a desperate need to stem the hostility of the students, which was increasing like the number of casualties, Vesta decided to go to the school herself. She had just stepped onto the platform to appeal for calm when the police stormed the building and the students scattered. Chased by the police, some of the students were brutally beaten with heavy truncheons and others were shoved bleeding and screaming into waiting police vans. Vesta herself was arrested and subsequently charged under the Riotous Assembly Act, and she received a suspended sentence. A short time after that, and without explanation or reason, she was arrested again and locked up under the Internal Security Act. The Act enabled the government to detain anyone indefinitely, without trial and without any intervention by the courts.

'It was a Friday afternoon and I was working at SACHED when they came for me. Our director asked them if they were going to put me in solitary confinement. The policeman replied that I would be going in with all the other women. As they were driving me to the prison, I had the hope that I was going to be with other women, but when we got to the prison, which we called the "Fort", the gate opened and there was no one else about. When I stepped out of the van all I could see was a yard with rows of doors encased within stark grey stone walls. They took me to a cell which could not have been more than four or five feet wide with a very high ceiling. I was completely thrown off balance because I thought I would walk into this place and say, "Hello folks," but there was no one there. I was devastated and confused and just couldn't take the isolation.

'During the night, as I stood in complete darkness, there was a knock on the wall and a voice called out, "Is anybody there?" I answered and told her my name. She then shouted at the top of her voice, "Vesta Smith is here." She told me that her name was Si Bongile. I felt her warmth through those cold grey walls and was comforted by it. I told her that I couldn't sleep, that I wasn't prepared for prison and was frightened. Then Si Bongile, this child, this very small person, began to sing to me. She had a beautiful voice which lifted my spirit. I was relieved to know that someone was next to me with such compassion. I moved to the mat in the corner of my cell and allowed myself to sleep. Si Bongile sang to me every night, though we never saw each other for about three months.'

The cruelty of the prison regime was designed to cause the maximum amount of psychological damage to the women, not only by cutting them off from human contact but also by restricting any view of the world outside. The small window set high up in the cell wall allowed only a limited amount of light through the grimy glass, and the warders even made certain that nothing and no one could be seen through the keyhole by blocking it from the outside.

'We had two identical pots in our cells. One was for the toilet and the other for water to drink. In the morning I would be escorted out from my cell to empty out my pots.

'They were then taken away from us and returned later on, and it was impossible to know which one had been used for the toilet and which one was for the water. Because of that, I stopped drinking water from the pot. The ordinary inmates would bring us water to wash ourselves. During the day, we were allowed half an hour of exercise, which was to walk up and down on our own in the prison yard before being taken back to the cell. The next prisoner was only allowed out once you were back inside, to make sure that we didn't see each other.'

Solitary confinement took its toll on Vesta. She thought constantly of her family outside and how they were coping without her. The only reading matter allowed in the cell was a bible provided by the prison authorities. This was not peculiar to South Africa: a century before, the same 'penitent' philosophy had been used in the jails of the United States. The theory was simple: leave a prisoner in solitude with a bible and it would only be a matter of time before he or she read it, saw the error of their ways and recanted. Vesta did not read the bible – their God was not her God – but she did pray.

'After I resigned myself that there was nothing I could do, a gentle and warm feeling came over me and I felt at ease. It was as though there was a presence, but I can't explain it, I just had this feeling that I was no longer alone.'

In its eagerness to remove activists from their communities, the government failed to formulate a coherent strategy for dealing with political prisoners like Vesta. The prisoners, most of whom could not be charged with any offence, received unpredictable and contradictory treatment from the prison authorities. They were subject to the same strictures as criminal inmates, yet were allowed to wear their own clothes; they were in solitary confinement, but could receive visits from friends and relatives.

In the midst of such anomalies, Vesta was determined to maintain a spiritual and emotional wellbeing, but she suffered physically. The strain of imprisonment impaired her appetite and she could eat only very little of the food brought to her by her daughters, Cecilie, Inez and Bertha, during their twice-weekly visits. Vesta continued to lose weight until Cecilie was also imprisoned. Three months after her initial incarceration, the other prisoners implored Vesta to eat more so that she could be strong for Cecilie, who was pregnant with her third child and was suffering badly from diarrhoea.

'By the time Cecilie came in we were allowed to sit together from nine until twelve. We would play cards and games and talk. I would sit in the yard and aeroplanes would pass very low overhead. I watched these planes, knowing that my children, my mother and my family were seeing them too. We were seeing something together; the planes were a connection between myself and those I loved in the outside world. Even today if I see a plane I will stop and watch it. People may think that I am mad, but in a strange kind of way they helped me to survive in prison and I still have a fascination with them.'

Amnesty International and several other bodies began to express their concern about the conditions in which prisoners in South Africa were being held and put pressure on the authorities for change.

'For months, during the cold winter, we had been sleeping on thin mats on a cement floor with just a blanket to keep us warm. Then, one day, we were suddenly told to get out of our cells and stand by our doors. We had no idea what was going on until we saw the ordinary inmates carrying mattresses into our cells. One prisoner said that the International Red Cross must be coming to pay a visit. She was defiant and refused the mattress at first, wanting the true conditions to be seen, but like everyone else she was forced to comply. Sure enough, the International Red Cross came and they found us on beds that were as big as the cells. That night I got onto the bed and was able to see through my window for the first time. I screamed to the girls to get onto their beds and look out of their windows. There was a full moon, and it was the first time that we had seen the moon and the stars in four months. I remember the applause and cheers that rang through the prison at seeing something we had so often taken for granted. It was beautiful.'

The relaxation of the harsh regime, and the improvement in their living conditions, provided a new impetus for the women to find their voices and gain strength from each other. Their confidence grew, and it was not long before they were challenging the way the prison operated.

'The black warders called the white warders "Nona", which means "madam", and the white warders referred to the black warders as "Vakashi" , which means "Visits". We never quite understood why the black warders were called "Visits" but we told them that, as they were employed by the government, whether they were black or white they were all "Nonas" or they were all "Vakashis". If they couldn't agree to this, they should call each other by their names.

'One day, we were called into the office by the head of the prison. She was a strapping white woman with a lot of yapping dogs around her legs, and she said to us that she didn't know why the Security Branch chose to bring us to her prison as we had caused so much upset. The second time I was in prison, there were no Vakashis or Nonas and so I guess our message had got through.'

Of course, there were many things about South African prisons that Vesta and her colleagues could not change. 'The ordinary white inmates were given much better treatment and had comfortable cells with furniture. The black inmates were ordered to wait on them as if they were servants and refer to them as "Madam". To be kept busy, the black women prisoners also had to scrub the tarred yard with hand brushes. This was a pointless and laborious task, especially in the summer when the tar would soften.

'One day we watched a young woman, an ordinary inmate, who was making her way across the yard. She was in some difficulty and barely able to put one foot in front of the other. We asked her what was the matter and she explained, in tears and embarrassment, that she was having a period but had no panties to keep her sanitary towel in place. We knew that the uniforms for ordinary inmates included panties and so we elected a spokesperson to see the superintendent and complain about this young woman's plight. She was given several excuses about why the inmate had not been issued with underwear, but she refused to believe or accept any of them and implored that warders attended to her needs. The next day the young woman strode toward us with a big smile on her face and pulled up her uniform to show us that she had been given a pair of panties.

'We all cheered. It was a small victory, but also a great one because we had helped to preserve the dignity of one of our sisters.'

Probably to the great relief of the prison authorities, Vesta and Cecilie were released on 22 December 1976, shortly after the ending of the students' actions, which had left at least 575 dead at the hands of the security forces. Although they were released into a period of relative calm, it was not long before they resumed their roles in the struggle.

A few months after her release, Vesta and her friend Oshadi Mangena were appointed to serve on a committee that was to enable different regions to liaise with a clinic in King William's Town. The Zanempilo Clinic had been set up by Steve Biko, his friend Peter Jones, and his partner,

Mamphele Ramphele, and acted as the centre for the Black Consciousness Movement, which promoted a positive self-image for black South Africans.

'For Steve, if you were not white, you were black and this is something that I have been trying to tell my people. When Steve was talking about the black African, he included so-called coloureds and Indians. This notion of black was what Steve taught me. I never saw it in that light until he started his Black Consciousness Movement and then I saw it as it should be. I would always say to people, "Fine, you are so-called coloured, you are the middle of the sandwich but when it comes down to brass tacks, the whites will throw you in with the blacks." In the past, for example, the post offices had white entrances and non-white entrances. On the trains there could be nine out of eleven carriages reserved for whites and the remaining two for non-whites. So then I would ask them, "How is it that so-called coloureds could think that they were really treated better than the African person?"

'Steve was also adamant that we should not stick to the white man's way of doing things; he wanted us to completely change our way of thinking. I remember when we were discussing a complaint about one person who was misusing the car we had for the clinic. I, as the older person, and thinking about what we would have done at the city council, said that we should get a sort of register so that we could keep tabs on him. Steve was very cross and shouted at me. He said, "How dare you bring in what the white man would do? We won't do that, we will find another way."

'I was shocked at his outburst, but understood his anger at a method which he thought might create mistrust among us. An element of apartheid.'

Despite being harassed, taken in for questioning and on several occasions held in detention for periods of one or two days, Vesta refused to be deflected from the struggle.

Three months after it was set up, she joined the Legal Resources Centre (LRC), in Johannesburg. The LRC had been established by Arthur Chaskalson, who had been a member of the team that defended Nelson Mandela and the other leaders of the ANC at the Rivonia Trial of 1963–4 and who was later to become president of the Constitutional Court following the election of the country's first truly democratic government; the LRC's other founding members were Geoffrey Budlender, Charles Nupen and Felicia Kentridge. Vesta and Cecilie joined this group of white liberal lawyers to help provide legal advice and assistance to people from the townships.

In September 1984 a fresh wave of violence swept through the townships, leaving at least twenty-six people dead and three hundred injured. Six months later, in March 1985, a second cycle of violence, even more intense and prolonged, began in the townships of the Eastern Cape.

Surprisingly, Vesta was able to secure travel documents that allowed her to leave South Africa for the first time in twenty years. Her last trip had been to see her sister in Zambia, and her visit had drawn the attention of the South African Security Services.

'It was just before the elections in 1969. My house was being used as the headquarters of the election campaign for the Labour Party, which was advocating equality for everyone. I looked through my bedroom window and saw a white man and a white woman coming to the door. The man introduced himself as Mr Smith and said he worked in Pretoria. He told me if I needed a passport he could give it to me, provided that when I next visited Zambia I would tell him what the ANC were doing there. I asked him if he was expecting me to spy on the ANC. He said that I wouldn't be spying but that I would be doing something for my country. I told him I didn't have a country because I didn't have a vote. He said that I should think about all my children, and that he could provide me with a big house and a big car, but I told him no thank you. I am sure that ended my chances of having a passport.'

Although Vesta was aware of the immediate consequences of refusing Mr Smith's offer, it was not until a few years later that she found out the full repercussions of her refusal.

After unsuccessfully applying for a passport annually for twelve years, Vesta at last received one in 1985, and in July she travelled to Nairobi where she met Oliver Tambo. A Catholic women's group called The Grail had sponsored her trip. During a press conference in Kenya, she realized that members of the South African Secret Service were in the audience.

'I knew they were there spying on us but that wasn't going to stop me from speaking the truth about the terrible things that were going on in South Africa and speaking up against the government's actions.'

Her suspicions were confirmed during her arrest and interrogation the following year: the police produced a photograph of her with Oliver Tambo.

Two months after getting her passport, Vesta travelled to Europe, including Britain and Ireland, giving talks and explaining to anyone who would listen about the suppression of the people of the townships and the terrible price they were paying in blood.

The South African government was not about to forgive or forget Vesta and shortly after her return home she was arrested yet again, this time with her three sons.

'It was two o'clock in the morning on 12 June 1986 when there was a terrible knocking on every window and every door in the house. I sat up in bed just as five policemen came into my bedroom. My stomach turned and I said a prayer. A policeman took hold of me and shook me. He said, "What are you doing? Are you praying? Communists don't pray." I said to him, "Of course I am praying, and I am not a communist, I am a Christian." The policeman's attitude changed immediately, and he stood back and told me to get dressed and collect my toiletries. One of the amazing things about some Afrikaners was that they seemed to have a fear of God. Judging from his reaction, it was as if my praying to God would put this policeman at risk of being struck down at that very moment.'

The plight of her sons preoccupied Vesta while she was incarcerated. 'Day and night I worried, and at one time I broke down because I knew how the prison warders treated the men. I found myself thinking about poor Steve Biko and how he had died. The authorities tried to say that he had taken his own life but anyone who knew Steve dismissed this as a lie. I remember he used to say that if you go into prison, whatever they give you eat it, even if it is shit. Don't let them get you down. Keep up your strength. Don't even let them see you cry. Every day my boys were in prison was a great worry to me.'

Fortunately, the LRC, the very body Vesta had helped to make so effective, came to her aid and procured her release and that of her sons. Later, it even obtained compensation for her sons' wrongful arrest and detention. This was a triumph – albeit a small one – which before 1979 would not have been possible for people without considerable financial means.

The latter 1980s were years of momentous change in South Africa, starting with the release of the ANC leaders from Robben Island. Vesta met her friend Walter Sisulu on the day of his release on 15 October 1989, but she did not meet Nelson Mandela until a month after he walked to freedom in February 1990. She was relieved to find him in such good health and happy to know that he remained the same open, warm-hearted person who had once given lifts to people from Soweto in his car. 'I was at the offices of the Legal Resources Centre when Nelson walked in. I was so surprised that he remembered me after all those years. But he just looked at me and said, "Hello, Vesta," and gave me a big hug. He asked about my mother and my sisters and I thought to myself, "This is a wonderful man." '

The days of fear of arrest, detention and interrogation are over. But for Vesta, the struggle continues. There are mundane as well as profound issues for her to confront in the new South Africa.

'You can tell when it is nearing election time, because the township becomes very clean. This morning, as I was calling on a neighbour, I saw a woman coming from the top of the road with rubbish to throw in the area that had just been cleaned up. I said to her, "Now that you have come to put your rubbish here, don't you think other people will do the same thing?" I asked her if she did not want to live in a clean place, but she looked at me as if I was mad. You have to try and make people feel proud to be an inhabitant of Noordgesig, and it starts with little things like not throwing rubbish around the place.'

A more profound issue is that of continuing racial prejudice, and for those outside of South Africa the source of that prejudice may be surprising. The marginalization of the so-called coloureds now being carried out by the Africans is not only perplexing but especially painful for one who has given so much of her life to the struggle for freedom and equality.

'I was sitting in the office of the welfare department and the chap in charge was ignoring anybody who could not speak an African language. He continued to call several people who had arrived after me until I got furious and confronted him in his own language. I had been pretending not to understand what was being said, just to see how far he would go. After a while I could no longer contain my anger and I told him what I thought of the way he was treating the so-called coloured people. He tried to get a bit stroppy with me but when he realized I was speaking his language and I said I was going to his boss, the minister, Geraldine Fraser-Moleketi, herself a so-called coloured woman, he backed down. I speak several African languages and it makes me sad to listen to the demeaning comments passed by blacks about the so-called coloureds. If we were favoured in the past by the white man it was not our doing. The only thing was to fight and get the injustices corrected so that everybody was treated equally.'

Equality still seems a rare commodity in the new South Africa. Recognition of their part in the struggle continues to elude not only some so-called coloured people but also other large sections of South African society. For example, during the liberation struggle thousands of women stood alongside the men and played their full part. Women took risks, suffered the most painful of times, were the sole support base, hid people on the run and kept their secrets. When men, some of them little more than boys, from the ANC were killed during border incursions, it was the women who travelled to collect their bodies and comfort their families. Yet very little has been written about their role in the liberation of South Africa. There is even less comfort when these women see some of the people who played a smaller role reaping many material benefits of post-apartheid South Africa. For them there remains a lasting sorrow. One that could easily be rectified by a recognition that they too played their part.

Vesta is quiet for a few moments as she remembers some of her comrades in the struggle. 'There are many thousands of women from South Africa that the world should know about. Wonderful and courageous women like Nomaindia Mfeketo, who is now the mayor of Cape Town, Jean Nowel from Durban, Lilian Ngoyi and Si Bongile.'

For countless men and women in the townships, the prospects remain bleak. Unemployment, alcohol and drug abuses are prevalent among men in the poor areas.

'Right around the township, you will find that men are often too drunk to help themselves. That for me is a challenge, and if I could I would arouse the consciousness of the women in my area to get the men off their backsides. We need to do that, because I just cannot see what is going to happen here without men taking a more positive and active part in the life of our communities. There is a real danger that, in the words of Steve Biko, they will become the shadows of men, completely defeated and drowning in their own misery.

'Women hold the key to the future. In this society women cannot merely help themselves, they have to support their men as well as their families. If you look at the minibuses travelling around Soweto, you will see that the majority of the passengers going to and returning from work are women.'

In her seventy-eighth year, Vesta is still working. She has established a women's group in Noordgesig. It meets once a week and is working to combat physical and sexual abuse within families.

'I am running a legal advice office because of my experience at the Legal Resources Centre. I am a sort of paralegal and I give legal advice to women who are suffering abuse. We haven't even got a little place to use as an office, so I do this work from my home. Today I may say, "Ah, I am not going to be involved in anything like this any more. I am tired." But tomorrow I may see a woman running down the street being chased by a man and I have to jump in. I can't give up – it is like opium. That is what it is.'

Jean Nowel reflects upon her relationship with Vesta.

'I met Vesta Smith (Ma V, as we all call her) more than thirty years ago. I was immediately struck by her strength of character, her dedication to ending the struggle of the oppressed in South Africa, and her hatred of apartheid. We struck up a strong and binding friendship and, more than that, we became family. My children are hers, her children and grandchildren are more like my brothers and sisters. I am both her daughter and her friend.

'She has an indomitable spirit and stands up against injustice wherever she may find it, regardless of the consequences to herself, even if she is a lone voice.

'For woman of her age, the amount of activity she packs into a day is unbelievable. She has a strong belief in herself, her worth as a human being, and she bows her head to nobody. She has helped me many times to walk, talk and be proud. One of her most endearing features is that she is just an ordinary black woman. Yet she is a true role model. She is an inspiration which makes you say, "If Ma V can do it, so can I, or I will do it because Ma V asked me." She is a very difficult woman to refuse. One of the true tragedies of our present South Africa is that heroes like Ma V are not recognized or appreciated for the true gems that they are.

'Although Ma V never expected or wanted recognition or rewards for her labours, the powers that be – and indeed the whole country – are the poorer for not using her powerful personality and dedication in building the country.

'One day I came back from visiting Ma V and told my family that she was not well, and for the first time, I could see that she was ageing. My son Alban said, "Oh God, please do not let Ma V die now. She is my role model, my inspiration and my guiding light. My life would be the poorer if Ma Vesta was not around." My sentiments exactly.

'Indeed, the day Ma V leaves us, as she must, a light will go out in my life. Just to know that she is here, in the same world as me, even though I do not see her as often as I would like, is consolation to me. The thought of her brightens my day and I thank God for her, daily.'

Vesta Smith's life has been one of courage and determination, often punctuated by sorrow and with a few all-too-brief moments of triumph. As a consequence of her meeting with Mr Smith in 1969, six years later the National Intelligence Agency planted a story within the upper echelons of the South African Council of Churches (SACC) that she had been working for the Security Service as an agent. To this day, the SACC's response, which was to dismiss her, brings a rare show of emotion. It is one that suggests she feels betrayed by people with whom she had worked for seven years. They had too readily accepted the accusations levelled against her. During 1975 there was yet another explosion of protests and brutal suppression by the state. The atmosphere was emotionally charged and, had the SACC's decision been made during the period when the 'necklacing' of people accused of being informants was rife, it could have cost Vesta her life.

Vesta endured the suffering meted out by the barbarous apartheid regime but there was also great pain in her personal life. In 1963 she married Leslie Smith but his alcoholism made the marriage short-lived. It is an episode that Vesta bore stoically. But for all the rigours in a lifetime of tremendous hardship, it was the sudden and unexpected death of her foster-daughter Margaret that produced the most profound physical reaction. Margaret died from a stroke at the age of forty-four, while Vesta was in Europe in 1985. During the course of the night, the shock turned her hair from black to white.

Vesta had came into contact with Margaret and her older sister, Bertha, while she was working for Johannesburg City Council. Their parents had been killed in the great train crash of 1949, which left over two hundred people dead. After Bertha graduated from school, she gained a place at Wits University and was due to take up residence at the Douglas Smit Halls, the only accommodation available for black students. Having lived in hostels since the age of eleven, Bertha had grown weary of a life without a family and asked Vesta if she could live with her. Vesta agreed and also provided a home for Margaret, while her mother, Clara, took in Bertha's two brothers, Alfred and Abel.

Vesta Smith's life has been one of giving; she has never sought either wealth or fame, only justice. But perhaps the final words should be those of Arthur Chaskalson, president of the Constitutional Court and her colleague for fifteen years at the LRC.

'Vesta Smith is a remarkable person, a woman of great integrity, altruism and dignity. She is a warm and compassionate woman with a dry sense of humour who does not suffer fools gladly. She has always chosen to stand up for herself and for others. In this she has acted fearlessly. Where necessary, she expressed her views on public platforms. In apartheid South Africa, this involved considerable risk. Every aspect of her life has been consistent with her desire to see justice for all in South Africa.

'Vesta has never aspired to high office, wealth or status. She has lived a life of unusual and consistent principle in practice. Her life has not been materially easy, neither has it been without personal tragedy, but she has the strength to cope with and transcend adversity. Knowing her is a privilege and a pleasure.'

Cecilie Palmer

10   *Continuing the Journey*

Seated at her desk in the twelfth-floor office of the Women's Institute for Leadership Development and Democracy (WILDD) in the centre of Johannesburg, Cecilie Palmer is a slight but striking figure. Her skin is soft and blemish-free, belying her fifty-seven years, but there is something about her light-brown eyes which suggests that her life has been plagued with adversity. She swivels in her chair and draws on a cigarette, nodding as she listens attentively to the older woman sitting by her side. For the casual observer it would be hard to tell if the women are colleagues, old comrades in the struggle, friends, or mother and daughter. In fact, they are all those things and more.

Vesta Smith is only paying a short visit and after a few minutes she makes her way out along the narrow corridor. Her exit is not a speedy one; the women who put their heads round their office doors to exchange a few words delay her leaving and Cecilie looks on from her doorway, blowing blue smoke from her smiling lips. Her relationship with her mother is a complex one which cannot easily be characterized or understood.

It began in Noordgesig, a small township which was established south-west of Johannesburg as a transit camp during the Second World War. Clara Palmer, a superstitious woman, had pleaded with her daughter, Vesta, to do her best to delay giving birth until the following day. But in spite of Vesta's best efforts Cecilie emerged into the world at 11 p.m. on 13 May 1944.

'Unlucky thirteen, according to my granny,' laughs Cecilie, trying to create order from the piles of papers on her desk. 'She brought me up and was always very protective. Although I never really knew why, it might have been because I was an illegitimate child and had very little contact with my father, Cecil Noluntshungu. I only met him for a short time when I was six and then again when I was eighteen. He never really supported my mother or me. But my mother had a better relationship with the father of my brother, William, and my sister, Inez, because he was a lot more caring; his name was Welcome Smith. We all lived together for a while in my granny's house until my mother had saved enough money to buy her own house. They then moved as a family, but I stayed with my granny until the last year at boarding-school when I was thirteen. You could say that my upbringing was not a particularly normal one.

'I visited my mother but because I didn't live with her I could not feel that I was part of her family. In fact, I was more able to relate to my cousins who I lived with at my granny's house than to William and Inez. My relationship with them only developed much later in life.'

That separation played a part in developing a self-reliance in the young Cecilie, but other potent influences contributed to the way she perceived the world around her. First, there was the private education paid for by her mother that taught her independence but also, from a very early age, there was the insidious effect of a racism so pervasive that it was even present in her own family.

As she approached her teenage years, Cecilie learnt of the more subtle prejudices about skin colour and this growing awareness impacted most on her relationship with her grandmother.

'My granny was a light-skinned woman who didn't really like black people. As I got older I realized that there was a lot of racism in the things she said and did. I remember coming home one day from school with my hair plaited in cornrow. She screamed at me and asked how I could let my hair be plaited in that way when I must have known that it would make me look too African. She said that I should always look like a 'coloured' and never plait my hair like that again. Granny was snobbish and had little time for black people who did not have an education; she felt they were only fit to clean the house and to be servants. If you were an educated black person, she would accept you. I suppose that is why she married my grandfather: he was an educated, black African man.

'My grandmother did not have a formal education herself, but she read the newspapers every day and she was the driving force behind our local tenants' association. She also ran a crèche in the township, and most of the children from Noordgesig, regardless of their colour, attended. In spite of all her prejudices, she was a very calm and dignified woman and I dearly loved and admired her.'

At a time when the apartheid regime was actively separating so-called coloureds from blacks, the difference in colour within Cecilie's family created tensions which were deeply felt but rarely talked about. The Prohibition of Mixed Marriages Act was introduced in 1949; it was soon followed by the Immorality Act, which made sexual relationships between people from different ethnic groups illegal. Two more laws were passed in 1950: the Population Registration Act, which classified all South Africans according to race; and the Group Areas Act, which meant that each racial group could own land, occupy premises and trade only in its own separate areas. The human misery these laws caused is immeasurable. Families were uprooted and in some cases they were torn asunder if members were of different skin colours. Cecilie feared that this might happen in her own family.

'We were always the black part of the family because, even though two of my aunts were fair-skinned, my mother was a shade darker and my Aunt Esme was almost as dark as my grandfather. All my mother's cousins were lighter and had straight hair but we had kinky hair. Because I was afraid that at any time we might be separated, I felt it was better not to become too close to any of my family in case one day they were gone.'

In a society in which racism tainted every human activity, there was little respite from the emotional and physical consequences of apartheid. Even as a small child at school, Cecilie was exposed to many forms of institutionalized racism.

'When I was eight I went to the Little Flower boarding-school in Natal, which was run by Catholic nuns. Although they belonged to the same order, the white German nuns were all teachers and wore the traditional black and white habits; but the black nuns wore grey habits and worked in the garden, laundry or kitchen. This really bothered me, and it was only many years later that I thought that the way the nuns were organized could have been a product of racism.

'Although the Little Flower was a boarding-school for so-called coloured children, whose skin tones ranged from the fair to the very dark, there was a degree of prejudice that favoured those children with lighter skins.'

Cecilie pauses, and her eyes attest to the nature of the cruelties she both witnessed and endured. From her acute but deep silence one might guess that most of what she knows will remain unspoken. But one can also imagine that her experience bears witness to the everyday suffering of millions of people in apartheid South Africa who bore the brunt of an evil that went in the guise of 'separate development'. Children, the most vulnerable of its citizens, did not escape exposure to this malevolent doctrine; like their parents, they were subjected to a process designed to strip them of dignity and self-esteem.

'The nuns denounced any pride we felt as children after the Second World War that South Africa had played its part in defeating Nazism. By asserting that the Allies would not have won the war if the Russians had not intervened, they made us feel that we had nothing to celebrate. They often seemed to look for ways to undermine our confidence and self-esteem, and I thought this was cruel.'

Outside school there were constant reminders of her place as a 'coloured' girl in a white-dominated society. 'I remember when I used to go into town in my Sunday best with my mother. We went to the very exclusive shops. It was a real treat and something I always looked forward to. One day, my mother and I went into a shoe store where there was an adventure play area with a brightly coloured climbing-frame, swings, a slide and other play equipment. I looked at all the white children who were going up and down the slides and were being pushed on the swings, and wished I could join in. But for some reason I knew that I was not allowed to. My mother saw this and I remember her picking me up and defiantly putting me on one of the swings. She pushed me and then stood and watched as I took turns on every piece of apparatus. I thought that she was almost daring any of the store assistants to challenge us. No one did, but I often wonder what might have happened if they had.'

As a teenager Cecilie encountered the brutal impact of the hated Pass Laws on the African population. 'It was a blazing hot day and six African men, who were stripped to their waists, were unloading crates of Pepsi-Cola from a truck. A police van sped up to them. Dust rose from the ground as the van screeched to a halt. The police got out and began to jostle the men and demand that they produce their passes. They were unwilling to accept the men's explanation that they had left their passes in their jackets, which were back at the factory, and pushed them into the van and took them away. The men were only working hard to make a living for their families, and that was their crime.

Everyone who saw that happen knew that the men would be shoved through the courts and be made to pay ten rand. It was a lot of money in those days, and if they couldn't pay they would have to spend ten days in prison or work ten days on the potato farm in Bethal, providing cheap labour for the white farmers. I vaguely remember a potato boycott, when people decided that they would not eat potatoes because of how African men were treated on those farms.'

Although Cecilie did not become a victim of the Pass Laws, at the age of sixteen she was summoned to be classified under the 1950 Population Registration Act. It was humiliating to be instructed to parade in front of a panel of examiners before she was officially categorized as 'coloured'. The board of classification had, in theory, a range of categories available in Cecilie's case because of the light-brown shade of her skin: coloured; other coloured; Malay; or Cape coloured. Many people, including Cecilie, were unsure of the criteria that separated the 'coloured' people not only from black or white but also from other people who had been classified similarly. For those with a darker complexion there were two important tests: the thickness of one's lips and the constitution of one's hair. With regard to the latter, a matchstick was pulled through the hair to analyse its curliness, and it was on the basis of such arbitrary tests that it was decided where a person could live and work.

'I remember when I went with my mother to be classified and she had to give information about my birth and who my father was. I was crying as we left, because I not only felt degraded by the whole affair but was devastated to learn that my parents had never been married. I didn't tell my mother until years later how bad I felt that she was not married when I was born. For me it was a betrayal because, being at a Catholic school, I was sure all my friends' parents were married and it made me feel ashamed that my parents were not. I resented the feeling that there was something else different about me.'

By this time Cecilie was living with her mother, but despite the strong family tradition of academic achievement she did not finish high school. 'I lost interest in school, and on more than one occasion I was chased out of class because I was always falling asleep.

'I played truant for three months without my mother ever finding out. I would get on the train at ten past six in the morning, wait until I knew my mother had gone to work, and then catch another train to go back home, where I would laze about.'

Knowing it was only a matter of time before she was found out, Cecilie applied for early entry to a nursing career and at the age of seventeen she was accepted to train at the Coronation Hospital in Johannesburg. But, like her schooling, Cecilie's training-course came to a premature end and she managed to do only one year and nine months of a three-and-a-half-year course.

'I know I disappointed everyone, including the matron, who had gone out of her way to get me into nursing because I had not been old enough at the time of the intake. But I couldn't take the medical part of nursing when patients died. The surgical part was OK – you could fix people with broken bones – but I couldn't cope with dead people. I went on leave one afternoon and simply never returned.'

Cecilie's next career move changed the course of her life, despite an inauspicious beginning as a junior typist at Johannesburg City Council. She had done some typing at school but her rate, at only a few words a minute, was slow. Determined to increase her speed and accuracy, she bought herself a typing manual and practised for many hours after work. Her skills improved, and a year later she got a more challenging job: with the Students' Representative Council (SRC), at Witwatersrand (Wits) University, home of the National Union of South African Students, a body renowned for its anti-apartheid activities.

A fast learner, Cecilie was soon promoted to executive secretary to the president of the council; she had at last found a job which not only interested her but also gave her an active role in the struggle. 'It was an interesting time for me and I loved being a part of what was an energetic and indomitable group of young people. They looked to me to help plan and organize a number of student protests, which was something I enjoyed very much. I was one of a growing number of young activists on campus and, although what we were doing was dangerous, at that time we just didn't stop to think about the consequences.'

The perils of such activities became apparent when the police rounded up student leaders, including Charles Nupen (later a founder member of the Legal Resources Centre, where Cecilie and her mother both worked) and the president of the SRC, Glen Moss. But the security police also knew of Cecilie's involvement in the protests and felt certain she could provide them with enough information to secure convictions.

'I could not believe that the police really thought I would give evidence against those guys, but when I refused they decided to summon me to court. My mother, who had no idea about what I was doing, was very anxious about the whole situation and offered me a plane ticket to neighbouring Botswana, where she urged me to go into exile. By this time I had two young children and a life without fear of incarceration was appealing. But then I thought that being in exile was too permanent. And if we were all to run away, who would remain to fight? Instead I packed a few things and travelled to Natal in a battered old Volkswagen to stay with friends until things settled. A few weeks later my son Kim became very ill with broncho-pneumonia and I had to return to Johannesburg so that he could get the right medical treatment. When I arrived home the security police were waiting outside my flat with a notice for me to go to court the next day. I pushed past them and, holding on to my sick child, told them that if they wanted me in court they would have to come and fetch me. The next day three of them arrived and I had to go with them.'

Even though she knew she faced a possible eighteen-month jail sentence, Cecilie remained defiant as she went to court, determined not to give any evidence that would incriminate her colleagues. But shortly after her arrival the possibility of imprisonment receded, because a technicality, one of disclosure, meant that the case against her collapsed. Cecilie walked free from court but she knew that from then on she would be under surveillance by the security services.

Undaunted by the risk, the following year, 1975, Cecilie established the Institute of Black Studies with her friend and mentor Nimrod Mkele in Braamfontein.

'Nimrod and I set up the Institute because we wanted an organization which was bold enough to tell the truth about what was really happening in South Africa and how black people were suffering. There was a need for a voice for the truth as we saw it, and not the wishy-washy stuff that was pouring out of places like the Institute of Race Relations. We wanted a place where black people would feel safe to talk to each other.

'As a way of promoting the Institute, Nimrod and I organized a conference. The day before the conference was to take place it was banned by the police. This wasn't going to stop us and so we literally moved the conference out of Johannesburg – and their jurisdiction – to the Wilgerspruit Fellowship Centre in Roodepoort. It was a great success and attracted prominent activists such as Mamphele Ramphele, Njabulo Ndebele and Jakes Gerwel. We talked, shared experiences, listened to what was happening in other provinces and discussed strategies which would help ease the turmoil in our lives. We drew great strength from each other and there was a solidarity that gave us hope.'

The euphoria surrounding the success of the conference came to an abrupt end when, a few days later, the police raided Cecilie's office, confiscated numerous documents, including the conference papers she had been working on, and arrested her. Although she was mentally prepared for her arrest Cecilie was caught off guard in one very important aspect. Activists against the apartheid regime were under constant threat of arrest once the authorities knew them, and Cecilie had often advised women involved in the struggle always to be ready for such an eventuality.

'I was one of those activists who urged women always to be prepared, and carry a spare pair of panties with them at all times in case they were arrested. Yet when the police came for me I wasn't carrying an extra pair. At first, I was more angry about that than about being arrested.'

That initial anger soon faded and fear took its place as she was taken to the police station in John Vorster Square in the centre of Johannesburg. The police station was notorious because of the number of activists who had 'slipped' and cracked their heads, or had mysteriously fallen from a window on the ninth or tenth floor.

'I remember this big, stocky cop who was with us in a room on the tenth floor at John Vorster Square as we were waiting to be transferred to prison. He looked at me with hate in his eyes and said, "You people say that for every one of you that we kill, you will take one of us with you. Well, I say that I will have taken hundreds of you people with me by the time I am finished and shall still be happy to meet with St Peter at the Pearly Gates." Knowing how easy it would have been for me to have "fallen from a window" as so many others had done, I didn't react to his threat. Instead I looked out of the window and decided to accept my fate. I thought about my children and, once I had satisfied myself that they would be looked after, I wasn't afraid to die.'

Pregnant with her third child and suffering terribly from diarrhoea, Cecilie was taken to the prison. 'I was feeling very sick but Vesta was there and she and the other women rallied around and helped me a great deal.'

It is always 'Vesta', never 'Mother' or 'Ma'.

'Vesta and I are two very independent people. In a sense we are so different that I don't think we will ever be close. We love and will support each other in a crisis but I never call her "Mother". When I was at boarding-school I would write "Dear Mummy", but I would never say it to her face. I could never tell her any of my problems, even though I am sure she would do everything in her power to help me. We can hug each other and hold hands sometimes but there is always an uneasy calm between us. Vesta is a remarkable woman but I have never felt under her shadow because I have managed on my own and prefer to work things through myself. I guess I saw my grandmother as more of a mother figure and this might have been difficult for Vesta.'

In 1979 Cecilie began to work with the newly established Legal Resources Centre (LRC) in Johannesburg, which had been set up by her old friends Charles Nupen and Geoff Budlender together with Arthur Chaskalson and Felicia Kentridge. Cecilie was instrumental in bringing Vesta to work at the LRC, and they worked there together for many years.

Cecilie has many fond memories of her time at the LRC, the highlight of which was the visit of Nelson Mandela shortly after his release. 'There was great excitement when he arrived, and of course many of his old friends were there including Arthur and Vesta. When the excitement died down we all went back to our offices and then, after about fifteen minutes, there was a knock at my door. It was Nelson, who told me that my mother had sent him to collect the envelope she had left on the desk for my Aunt Esme. I gave it to him and he said, "Thank you." It made me smile to think that only Vesta Smith could have sent someone who was destined to become a world icon on such an errand.'

In 1994 Cecilie left the LRC and with three friends established the Women's Institute for Leadership Development and Democracy (WILDD).

'Things were changing fast when the end of apartheid came and we knew at some stage we, as women, were going to have to educate ourselves. We were going to have to learn many new skills to survive and we would have to learn them together. The reality for women was different from that of the exiles who were flooding back into the country, a lot of them with university degrees. Many women who had stayed in South Africa, particularly the older ones, did not have time to get a formal education. Our fight for freedom took priority over everything else.

'It was the women who were out there smuggling young activists out of the country when their lives were in danger, who protected others from arrest and brought back the bodies of the young men who were murdered and left on the side of the road like dead animals. We women went into open warfare for our right to be treated as human beings; we did things that we hadn't been prepared for.

'We were the messengers when organizations like the United Democratic Front were banned. We held strategic meetings, prioritized what needed to be done and got messages to the menfolk. We were called out in the middle of the night and, leaving our children in their beds, went to urgent rallies or meetings. Our homes were never private; they were open houses for anyone who needed help. We were always busy because there were things to do. We learnt to do them properly because we knew they were dangerous.'

Cecilie draws her fingertips across her cheeks to prevent

the tears rolling down her face as she adds, 'Our lives have been one perpetual struggle, which also involved bringing up a family, often single-handedly, in the midst of a cruel system. No one but ourselves could prepare us to live in the new South Africa.'

During the liberation struggle many women found themselves performing arduous feats they had never thought possible. For some it was finding the strength to roll boulders in front of oncoming police vehicles; and, as she recalls with a smile, in Cecilie's case it was discovering she had the agility to jump a six-foot fence in a single leap.

'It was during a student protest in 1983. Women were always out there with the young people to try and protect them and make sure that there were lawyers on hand in case any of them were picked up. I had made the mistake of going to the picket dressed in a pair of jeans and a T-shirt. It was a mistake, because I would have had a better chance of challenging the police if I had been in a skirt but dressed as I was I could easily be mistaken for a youth. When the police charged I thought it was best if I ran with [the students]. A few jumped the fence and, much to my surprise, I followed.'

Cecilie is quick to point out that the struggle for freedom did not always necessitate putting oneself at risk of imprisonment or physical danger: there were many ways of campaigning for reform. 'We once promoted "Black Christmas" by urging people not to go into the shops and spend money. Because the cops were everywhere we had to post our leaflets, and one night a few of us sat up until the early hours addressing hundreds of envelopes with names we got from the telephone directory.'

That flexible approach to problem-solving is one of the abiding principles underlying WILDD's aim to empower and educate the economically and socially disadvantaged women of South Africa. In many ways, WILDD is a natural progression from the Eldorado Park Women's Group that

Cecilie had helped set up during the liberation struggle. At that time it was beneficial to be seen as apolitical, and the group ran a pre-school and youth programme, a women's co-operative, a children's rights committee and a shelter for abused women. 'The majority of people who attended school meetings were women, and it was through our pre-school activities and parents' committee that we were able to politicize women in a legitimate and non-threatening way.'

The pre-school concept was soon adopted by groups in other provinces and provided a pool of recruits for WILDD. 'In 1993 we called all the women activists we knew and invited them to a consultative conference. We told them we had an idea to sell – and we sold it!'

With funding from a Swedish foundation, Cecilie and her colleagues began to recruit workers for WILDD. Wanting to utilize the skills and experience of the women they had worked with during the struggle, they contacted those who were known to be without jobs and took on thirty field workers. As a movement, WILDD was going to help promote women's leadership and involvement in South Africa's fledgling democracy, and the field workers needed to be trained in leadership and political campaigning.

'We already knew many of the women we recruited. They were strong, committed women who could be trusted. Some of them we had hidden with in the forest when we were on the run from the police. We paid them well and tried to find ways of compensating other women for the work they did. We were not prepared to use women as volunteers. Volunteering is a luxury many black women in South Africa could not afford.'

The advent of WILDD was not universally welcomed and there were those in positions of power who questioned the need for such an organization and wondered if it had been established to compete with the ANC's Women's League.

For Cecilie and her colleagues WILDD was about women's

activism in its entirety. A women's movement that was going to meet women's needs: not just talk about welfare, jobs or education, but ensure that women were properly represented on all structures, involved in decision-making and input into the debate around equality.

'When we first started, there were people who knew of our capabilities from the days when we were with the Federation of Transvaal Women. Because of this, I think a few of them chose to ignore us while others were a little afraid of us. We would see some women who were members of the Executive Council for Gauteng Province who had been with us in the "trenches". They would greet us with a hug, ask how we were, give us their cards and urge us to call them. But when we called and left messages, our calls were never returned or our messages responded to. After a while we stopped calling because, after all we had been through, we were not going to let ourselves be disrespected in this way. Now they are calling us because they need help and support for some of their programmes. We are responding, because we owe it to the women of our country who deserve a better life. We have to work with existing structures which will allow this to happen, no matter what we feel about some of the personalities within those structures.'

The influence of WILDD's members has spread throughout South Africa. In the north-west the Masana Literacy Project and Legal Advice Centre have been established in Mortele, while in Itireleng the building of a primary school is up for tender. In the Eastern Cape WILDD have overseen the establishment of projects ranging from the production of traditional African garments in Nthathi, to the manufacture of school uniforms in Sinathemba; from the founding of pre-school facilities in Tisane to the setting up of pig-farming in Mpekweni. In the Northern Province there are also literacy and legal advice projects. Port Elizabeth and Cape Town have two field workers, Nontobeko Fosilara and Ruth Mpekula, who have brought into existence two very strong groups which were engaged in the Advanced Political Training programme during 1998 and who are also involved with the Women Against Women's Abuse (WAWA) project.

The issue of violence against women had for years been lost in the atrocities of the apartheid regime. As the first buds of freedom emerged, it became apparent that South African society would have to come to terms with more than the violence that stemmed from an ideology of racial supremacy. WAWA support groups became very visible in every province and have proved a great support to the many women and children who looked to them for help. At a national level, WAWA began a campaign to ensure that the police are aware of the new Domestic Violence Act and that they co-operate in drafting further proposals to the provincial executive councils. In Johannesburg, WILDD has provided supervision for the WAWA project at Eldorado Park, which received a million-rand grant from the Department of Social Welfare, and has trained the lay counsellors at the Teddy Bear Clinic and the Child Welfare Society in their victim-empowerment programmes. The counsellors work at the Protea Court, helping children to get through court trials which have the potential to compound their harrowing experiences. Because of WILDD's involvement with the counsellors, Cecilie was nominated to be part of the team that has the task of setting up twenty Sexual Offences Courts nationwide.

Once viewed with suspicion and hostility, WILDD has become one of the most respected women's organizations in Johannesburg, and it has worked to overcome the barriers of mistrust between itself and those who have similar objectives, particularly within the ANC Women's League. This developing co-operation has led to a number of successful campaigns on major issues such as violence against women.

'We came together against the Nazarek serial killer, who

had raped and murdered forty-three women. We went to see President Nelson Mandela because we wanted his personal support, and then we organized a big protest around the area where these terrible crimes were being committed. A week or so after our protest, the killings stopped and someone was arrested.'

Although WILDD is increasingly successful in the improvement of women's personal, social and economic circumstances, Cecilie is keen to maintain a focus on women's involvement in South Africa's democratic process. The key impediment to many women running for political office or working in government administration is lack of education, and in an attempt to address this deficiency WILDD organized a Development and Democracy Programme. It is designed for women who are interested in obtaining a place in government, and includes training-courses such as Networking for Political Gain; Lobbying and Campaigning; Effective Media Relationships; and Understanding Power.

The nature of power, and how it can be used or abused, is something that Cecilie has witnessed at close quarters.

'I learnt a lot from my time at the LRC and I admired people like Arthur Chaskalson. He used to say, "Don't call me Mr Chaskalson. We are working together here, and no one is above anyone else. Please call me Arthur." I watched how he and his colleagues operated and I felt privileged to have worked with people who had real power and influence and used it with humility, patience and forethought. Many of my thoughts and actions around power and leadership come from what I learnt at the LRC.'

Such knowledge and experience proved invaluable when Cecilie came up against one of the most powerful women in South Africa.

'I lived with Winnie Mandela for three months in prison. We had a stormy relationship because she was a part of the prominent contingent who wanted to control everything. I told her straight that we had to pull together and support each other without trying to get the better of anyone else. Things settled after that.

'Winnie Mandela is a beautiful woman with a powerful presence which is appealing to many people, particularly those in the informal settlements. Most people are in awe of her, but I never was and never will be. I am in awe of no one. It is one of those things I took from the LRC that have served me well over the years.'

WILDD is not affiliated to any political organization and believes that individual members have the right to belong to any party they choose. Over the years it has helped many women run for political office; field workers with political aspirations were encouraged, and those who decided to stand for election were asked to present plans showing how they would cope with their work while simultaneously managing their campaigns.

In the 1999 elections a number of field workers and members of WILDD were elected to provincial and national government. Many of them took up positions of leadership and became chairpersons of various committees or executive members of metropolitan councils. Most of those women, including a number from the ANC, attributed their success to WILDD's Advanced Politics programme.

'We are extremely proud that so many women were appointed to government but we also acknowledge that the ANC's policy of adopting a 30% quota for women in leadership positions was a major contribution. But we cannot be either too relaxed or satisfied with what has been achieved so far. There is a fear that, with the new demarcation of local government boundaries, women will again be second best in the coming elections. This is something that we will have to watch.'

*

Back at her home in Roodeport, Cecilie is at last able to relax in the house she shares with her brother, William, her three children, Robin, Kim and Nadine, and her eighteen-month-old granddaughter, Lyndsey. Lyndsey's mother is Nadine, Cecilie's youngest and the child she carried in her womb during her imprisonment.

Nadine watches attentively from the sofa and is captivated as the baby scampers across the polished wooden floor. Her expression is full of hope for the future of her child – but there is also a trace of apprehension.

Though too young to have much personal experience of the injustices of the past, Nadine is of a generation and ethnic background that face new challenges, and perhaps part of her apprehension is that little Lyndsey will also have to face them. She eventually averts her gaze and says, 'I know my mother, grandmother and many other women sacrificed and fought hard in many ways, so that we should not have to experience what they went through. For a short time I worked with some of the women at WILDD and heard their stories and I know we have a lot to be thankful for. People might say it is up to us, the next generation, to secure the future, but young people in South Africa don't even know if they have a future or, if there is one, what it holds for them.'

Unemployment, particularly among the young, is one of the government's greatest challenges. From the lack of opportunity to work many other social ills are spawned. As well as the unfulfilled – and sometimes unrealistic – expectations about what a new democratic government could deliver in such a relatively short time, for young so-called coloureds like Nadine and her brothers there is a new and unexpected source of discontent. Many believe that as far as the government and other institutions are concerned the 'coloured' person has become invisible and that South African history has become one of black and white – and nothing in between. To back up their argument that they are being steadily marginalized in the new South Africa they cite advertisements in magazines and on television, in which 'coloured' people rarely, if ever, appear.

In the 1960s, the apartheid regime introduced the Preferential Treatment Act, which allowed 'coloureds' jobs from which Africans were barred. To right that wrong the new democratic government introduced an affirmative action plan, but some 'coloured' people believe that they have become the victims rather than the beneficiaries of the scheme.

'Job adverts used to say, "Only whites need apply," ' explains Nadine. 'Now some of them say, "Only blacks need apply." The whites don't seem to mind, because they see it as affirmative action, but when 'coloureds' who see themselves as black apply they are asked if they speak Zulu.

'I am lucky that I have a job, but some young people I know think that it would be easier to find a job if they were to change their surname to an African one. At first we were not white enough, and now it seems we are not black enough.'

For those who sacrificed so much in order that there could be a free and just South Africa, such comments are painful to hear. And yet, for those who have dedicated their lives to the fight against inequality, the eradication of the apartheid regime is but one victory – a single battle in the war for justice: they know the struggle must continue.

For Cecilie Palmer the price she has paid in her personal life for her part in the war against apartheid is immeasurable. She talks only briefly of her relationship with the father of her children or of her short-lived marriage. Perhaps events of that kind, which have emotionally crushed countless others, pale into lesser significance when compared to the other painful experiences she has endured. Perhaps such pain is the price that freedom has demanded from many thousands of people in South Africa; if that is the case, Cecilie Palmer has paid her share in full.

Marley Fakier is one of the women who shared aspects of Cecilie's life during the struggle. She can provide a rare insight into the private as well as public life of Cecilie Palmer.

'I have had the pleasure of knowing Cecilie for the past fifteen years and, because of our close working and personal relationship we have enjoyed during this time, I have gained insight into the inner person that is seldom exposed to casual acquaintances.

'Cecilie has the ability to display a mask of bravado, creating the impression that she is a stern, no-nonsense and unfeeling person. I know her well enough to realize that this is just a façade to hide the ultra-sensitive and empathetic and caring person that she really is. On numberless occasions, I have been witness to the deep anguish she has suffered when seeing the misery of women and children or when women have betrayed the principles she upholds and is prepared to die for.

'Her leadership abilities have been displayed on two occasions: once when she persuaded an angry group of youths to refrain from killing someone they had identified as a police informer; and again when she stopped them setting a house on fire. Her composed and soft-spoken approach to leadership has often been seen as a weakness by some, and there have been many times when the very people whose cause she has championed have opposed and disappointed her.

'One of her most outstanding attributes is her unwavering loyalty to her friends and the people she cares for. I have been a fortunate recipient of this giving nature of hers. From the moment we became comrades in the struggle I could always rely on her support, whether it was in opposing the powers that be at the time or in fighting for the empowerment of women. Without her at my side I would not have had the confidence and the courage to carry on.

'I believe that a person who cries in private when others are experiencing hardship must be a deeply spiritual person. There have been many times when I have had to console Cecilie when she was shedding tears because of the suffering of others.

'In this world, where self-interest holds so much sway, Cecilie is the antithesis of those whose sole purpose is enriching themselves. I have yet to come across a person who gives as freely and as selflessly as she does. When others are in need, Cecilie Palmer goes without.

'She has had her fair share of trials and tribulations, but the way she conducts herself in these times of hardship and affliction is an example to others. Her suffering during the struggle, which included her incarceration while she was pregnant, is well known. On the home front she had to endure the pain as a single parent of seeing her son facing false criminal charges, being shot at and surviving two car accidents. And through all this her commitment to working towards the alleviation of the pain of others never wavered.'

'I am proud of my mother,' says Nadine, as she gathers Lyndsey into her arms, 'but it wasn't always that way. I went to a private school and had many friends of all races. As none of their parents were politically involved, they were not interested in talking about apartheid. I did not talk about it either, and sometimes I felt ashamed that my mother had been in prison.

'Now I can see things differently and I know that without the support of my mother, how difficult life would be. She is a brilliant woman.'

At the beginning of the twentieth century, Stephen Palmer made a decision to challenge the inequality and racial prejudice that surrounded him and his family; it was a decision that profoundly shaped the destiny of some of his children and grandchildren. As a new century dawns, the quest for justice is not yet complete. If it is left to Nadine, or Lyndsey, one day to continue that journey which began all those years ago, few women will be better equipped or prepared for it.